A LITTLE GIANT

REALLY, REALLY GROSS JOKES, RIDDLES & TONGUE TWISTERS

Michael J. Pellowski

STERLING INNOVATION

An imprint of Sterling Publishing Co., Inc.

New York / London
www.sterlingpublishing.com/kids

STERLING, the distinctive Sterling logo, STERLING INNOVATION, and
the Sterling Innovation logo are registered trademarks of
Sterling Publishing Co., Inc.

Library of Congress Cataloging-in-Publication Data Available

10 9 8 7 6 5 4 3 2

Published by Sterling Publishing Co., Inc.
387 Park Avenue South, New York, NY 10016
© 2010 by Sterling Publishing Co., Inc.
Distributed in Canada by Sterling Publishing
c/o Canadian Manda Group, 165 Dufferin Street
Toronto, Ontario, Canada M6K 3H6
Distributed in the United Kingdom by GMC Distribution Services
Castle Place, 166 High Street, Lewes, East Sussex, England BN7 1XU
Distributed in Australia by Capricorn Link (Australia) Pty. Ltd.
P.O. Box 704, Windsor, NSW 2756, Australia

Design by Mike Rivilis
Interior art © shutterstock.com

Printed in China
All rights reserved

Sterling ISBN 978-1-4027-6002-0

For information about custom editions, special sales, premium and
corporate purchases, please contact Sterling Special Sales Department
at 800-805-5489 or specialsales@sterlingpublishing.com.

To the two guys I know who love really gross jokes, Matt and Marty.

CONTENTS

Gross Gigglers. **5**

Tasteless Jokes **47**

Something Smells Funny **89**

Gag on These. **111**

Sick, Sick Snickers **147**

Raunchy Riddlers **189**

It's A Real Gas! **223**

Gross Us Out! **243**

Stomach Churning Chuckles . **307**

Yuck Yuks! **355**

Bathroom Riddlers **395**

Going Crazy **431**

Silent But Deadly Smiles . . . **457**

GROSS GIGGLERS

What did the toilet tank say to the toilet seat?

Stop putting yourself down all of the time.

* * *

What do you call a double dose of morning mist?

Dew-dew.

GROSS TWISTER
Fleet Father Fodder
flew farther than fast
Friar Feeny flew.

What feels awful and hits lots of home runs in the month of October?

Wedgie Jackson.

❋ ❋ ❋

Why was the Wizard of Oz mad at Dorothy's pet?

Because Toto did a no-no on the carpet.

Why did Attila go to the Laundromat?
He had to wash his dirty hunderwear.

✳ ✳ ✳

KNOCK! KNOCK!
Who's there?
Snot.
Snot who?
Snot nice to keep me waiting, so open
the door.

✳ ✳ ✳

Al: I take my dog for a
walk around the block
to do his business.
Sal: Do everyone a
favor and start a
home business.

7

What happened when the clumsy centipede fell off of the roof?

He broke a leg, leg, leg, leg, leg.

✳ ✳ ✳

KNOCK! KNOCK!

Who's there?

Warts.

Warts who?

Warts up, Doc?

Mr. English: Why are you hopping
around my house like that?
Mr. French: I have to go to the
bathroom really bad.
Mr. English: Well, skip to my loo!

✳ ✳ ✳

**What did Victoria tell Elizabeth
before she left on vacation?**
Be sure to pack plenty of queen
underwear.

✳ ✳ ✳

**What do you get if you drink tomato
juice and buttermilk?**
Pink vomit.

SICK DEFINITION
Chair—
a rump roost.

What do you get when pigs pick their snouts?

Ham boogers.

✳ ✳ ✳

What do you get if you cross a firefly with a bathroom?

A bug that glows potty.

Hansel: Ick! This forest is a filthy mess!
Gretel: It must be the home of the
Three Pigs.

❋ ❋ ❋

Where does dragon milk come from?
It comes from cows with very short
hind legs.

❋ ❋ ❋

**What do you call an outdoor
bathroom used by hippies?**
A far outhouse, dude.

❋ ❋ ❋

**What parasite cheers and blows a
horn at sporting events?**
A rootie-tootie cootie.

What do you call a pimple on a duck?

Zit down.

* * *

Show me a giant who punches a pod . . . and I'll show you some black-eyed peas.

* * *

Gag Writer: How would you like to buy twelve dozen disgusting jokes?

Comic: Sure. I can always use gross material.

Teacher: Remember this important rule, students. Do not. I repeat, do not put your fingers in your noses.

Student: Wow! This class has a strict picking order.

Fred: I used to install toilets for a living.
Ed: What happened?
Fred: I got fired for sitting down on the job.

What do you get if a sheep doesn't use deodorant?

Ewe stink.

Boy: What do I have to do to buy a tame skunk?

Pet Store Owner: Fill out an odor form.

GROSS TWISTER
Hugh Pugh's pretty fine
pine pews.

Son: Why did you buy me a mechanical dog, Dad? I wanted a real dog.

Dad: A mechanical dog is better. You never have to feed or walk it. Best of all, you don't have to housebreak a mechanical dog.

Son: Is that so? Well our mechanical dog just leaked oil on the carpet.

Officer: Lady, you're not allowed to walk your dog in this area of the airport.
Lady: Why not?
Officer: It's a doody free zone.

✳ ✳ ✳

Which famous cartoon dog smells awful?

Scooby Doo-Doo.

✳ ✳ ✳

KNOCK! KNOCK!

Who's there?

Peking.

Peking who?

Peking your nose is gross.

Paris: My mother had cosmetic surgery done on her face. Now she has a new nose.

Harris: Did you help her pick it?

What does an octopus spend a lot of money on?
　　Underarm deodorant.

NOTICE
Attention all sailors—
please use port-a-potties
while on shore leave.

An older sister was grossed out when she saw her younger brother wipe his runny nose on his shirt sleeve.

Sister: Ick! That's disgusting! How would you like it if I did that?

Brother: No way! Use your own sleeve.

19

What did the hungry shark say when it saw a swimmer's hand in the water?
Ah, finger food.

Who smells bad and is in charge of the passing years?
Farter Time.

✳ ✳ ✳

What does a witch say after she belches?
Hex-cuse me!

✳ ✳ ✳

What college did the Green Giant graduate from?
Pea U.

✳ ✳ ✳

What do you get when two giant rams meet head-on?
Really big butts.

KNOCK! KNOCK!

Who's there?

Wren.

Wren who?

Wren you gotta go, you gotta go.

✻ ✻ ✻

Why is it painful for a giraffe to throw up?

Because the vomit has to travel such a long, long way.

✻ ✻ ✻

Clem: Where is the nearest outhouse?

Zeke: Sorry. I'm not privy to that information.

Clem: I went to propane school.
Zeke: Did you graduate?
Clem: No. I couldn't pass gas.

✳ ✳ ✳

Matt: Yesterday my dad made Russian chili.
Pat: Why do you call it that?
Matt: Because after you eat it, you spend the entire night Russian to the bathroom.

✳ ✳ ✳

KNOCK! KNOCK!

Who's there?

Yukon.

Yukon who?

Yukon use the bathroom now.

GROSS PEOPLE DIRECTORY

Dougie Doody
Brad Odor
Ivanna Tinkle
Hugo Potty
Bebe Tushie
Ken I. Piddle
Lotta Bea Hoe
Hugh Stink
Winnie D. Poo

What did one vacuum say to the other vacuum?

Hey man! Our job really sucks!

Andy: I think someone gave the Energizer Bunny too much prune juice.
Randy: What makes you say that?
Andy: Because it just keeps going and going and going.

Cowhand: I grow twenty acres of oats to feed my herd of mustangs.
Farmer: That's a lot of horse crop.

What did Mother Air Rifle say to Father Air Rifle?

It's time to burp the B.B.'s.

✳ ✳ ✳

KNOCK! KNOCK!

Who's there?

Hive.

Hive who?

Hive gotta go read bad. Where's the bathroom?

✳ ✳ ✳

Who lives in Transylvania, is hairy, and wears tighty whities?

The Underwear Wolf.

KNOCK! KNOCK!

Who's there?

Queen.

Queen who?

Queen the litter box. It's gross.

Why did the pastry chefs go to exercise class?

Because their buns were too big.

✳ ✳ ✳

Gina: My mother nicknamed my little brother "Trouble" because he refuses to take a bath.

Tina: Is that so? Well, I think I smell trouble coming.

✳ ✳ ✳

Jim: This is my new dog, Chuck.

Tim: Does he do any tricks?

Jim: He sure does. Watch this. Up, Chuck!

Ann: Yuk! My gelatin dessert is green and slimy.
Fran: Relax. It's just Jell-O mold.

✳ ✳ ✳

Why did the hen sit on a sharp axe?
Because she wanted to hatchet.

✳ ✳ ✳

Which dinosaur is always barfing?
Tyrannosaurus Retch.

✳ ✳ ✳

What do you call an insane black bird?
A raven lunatic.

YUCKY YULETIDE HUMOR

What do you get if you deep-fry Santa Claus?
Crisp Kringle.

Girl: *That department store Santa smells bad.*
Boy: *Maybe he has B-Ho.*

What do you call someone who is afraid of Santa?
Clausetrophobic.

What's red and goes "Oh! Oh! Oh!"?
Santa Claus walking backwards.

KNOCK! KNOCK!

Who's there?

Missy.

Missy who?

Missy diapers smell bad.

How can you tell if a scarecrow committed a crime?

Check his DN-Hay.

❋ ❋ ❋

Farmer: Have you ever hunted bear?
Hunter: No. I'm too modest.

GROSS DEFINITION
Stink bombs—stomach warfare.

Two tomatoes raced across a railroad track. Along came a train. One tomato ran too slow. The tomato who ran fast looked back and yelled, "Hey you! Ketchup!"

KNOCK! KNOCK!
Who's there?
Liver.
Liver who?
Liver alone, she'll be fine.

Who wrote Messy Fairy Tales?
Dirty Hans Christian Anderson.

RAUNCHY RHYMES

Ooey Gooey was a worm,
a mighty worm was he.
He sat upon the railroad track,
the train he did not see.
Ooey Gooey was he!

✳ ✳ ✳

Birdie Birdie in the sky,
Don't drop whitewash
as you fly by!

Why did the fitness instructor take his baby into the bathroom?
It was time for his toilet training.

✳ ✳ ✳

What did one tired toilet say to the other?
I don't know about you, but I'm pooped.

✳ ✳ ✳

Mother: Couldn't you stop yourself from throwing up in public?
Son: I couldn't help it. It was a gut reaction.

NOTICE

A farmer who builds an
outhouse in a grassy field
usually ends up weeding in
his bathroom.

What do you call a baby chick in the bathroom?

Toilet Peeper.

What runs fast and has black spots and red bumps?

A cheetah with acne.

36

Mr. Jam: Someone help me. I have a terrible rash and it's starting to spread!

* * *

What did the paintbrush say to the aerosol can?
Say it, don't spray it!

* * *

What did the skunk say to the baseball pitcher?
I dare you to wiff me.

* * *

What do you get if you cross an icky bug, a cow, and a bank clerk?
A roach-moo-teller.

KNOCK! KNOCK!

Who's there?

Ooze.

Ooze who?

Ooze going to clean up this mess?

✳ ✳ ✳

What do you call a severely twisted rope?

A knot case.

✳ ✳ ✳

What sound do you get if you cross a chicken with a crisp rice breakfast cereal?

Snap! Cackle! Pop!

Spike: What position do you play on the football team?

Mike: I line up way behind the wide receiver and go out for passes.

Spike: Oh! So you're kind of a rear end.

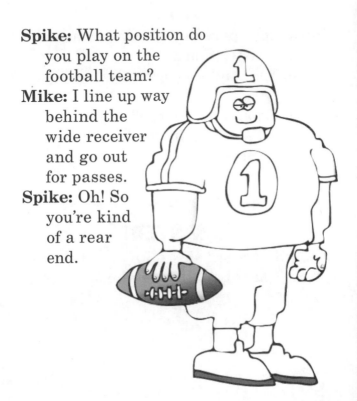

Sara: Your parents named your new baby sister Starr?

Lara: Yes. And she certainly lives up to it.

Sara: What do you mean?

Lara: All day long it's Tinkle, Tinkle, Little Starr.

TWISTER

Seth's six sick slimy snakes slowly slithered south.

KNOCK! KNOCK!

Who's there?

Urine.

Urine who?

Urine a lot of trouble.

❋ ❋ ❋

What do you get if you cross a cuddly yellow bear with a smelly skunk?

Winnie the Phew!

❋ ❋ ❋

Sheriff: The bank robbers are hiding in one of those many portable bathrooms. The question is, which one?

Deputy: Well, Sheriff, I guess we'll just have to flush them out.

41

What makes you laugh and itch at the same time?

The Flea Stooges.

✳ ✳ ✳

KNOCK! KNOCK!

Who's there?

Doughnut.

Doughnut who?

Doughnut spit on the sidewalk.

✳ ✳ ✳

Where did the outhouse finish in the bathroom race?

In turd place.

NOTICE
Acme Prune Juice
Company—it's easy to do
your business with us.

What buzzes around King Arthur's head?

The Gnats of the Round Table.

✳ ✳ ✳

What did Mr. Dog say to Mrs. Dog?

Why don't you kiss my barkside.

43

GROSS TWISTER

Polly's purple pooper scooper
sure scoops super.

KNOCK! KNOCK!

Who's there?

Gargoyle.

Gargoyle who?

Gargoyle with mouthwash, your breath
is bad.

What do you call a swarm of tiny shrimp lying along the highway?

Road krill.

* * *

Then there was the escaped convict who smelled so bad bloodhounds refused to follow his scent.

* * *

KNOCK! KNOCK!

Who's there?

Fun Gus.

Fun Gus who?

Fun Gus is growing on your feet.

How do you measure rubbish?
Use a junk yard stick.

✳ ✳ ✳

**What do you get if you cross
Godzilla with a centipede?**
A lot of squashed people.

TASTELESS JOKES

What's black and white with drops of red all over?

A sloppy penguin slurping tomato soup.

✳ ✳ ✳

What's black and white with drops of green all over?

A sloppy penguin slurping pea soup.

What do you get from rich, pampered cows?

Spoiled milk.

＊ ＊ ＊

Daughter: Mom, is this black bean soup?

Mother: No dear, it's clear broth. Why?

Daughter: Then there are bugs floating in my soup.

＊ ＊ ＊

Zeke: What kind of stupid snack are you eating now?

Clem: Beef jerky.

Son: What are we having for dinner
tonight?
Mother: Snails, so remember to eat
slowly.

✳ ✳ ✳

What do you call awful lemonade?
A bitter swill to swallow.

✳ ✳ ✳

Spike: I call this recipe
paddle boat chili.
Mike: Why?
Spike: Eat it and
it'll make your
stomach churn.

49

What kind of spicy chicken did Bill Cody like?

Buffalo wings.

* * *

Mother: Junior, use a knife to spread that on your toast.

Son: Calm down, Mom. I like having butter fingers.

* * *

Where does our planet digest its food?

In the bowels of the Earth.

* * *

What do you get when a messy person eats corn on the cob?

Corn on the slob.

Daughter: Mom, did you serve me raisin bran for breakfast?
Mother: No, why?
Daughter: Then there are bugs in my cereal.

＊ ＊ ＊

Al: My dad cooks a lot of greasy food.
Sal: It sounds like he's on a frequent fryer plan.

＊ ＊ ＊

Customer: Why do you call this steak the locomotive special?
Waiter: Because you have to chew, chew, chew every bite!

Mr. Frog: I only eat houseflies.
Mr. Toad: There's nothing like
homemade meals.

✳ ✳ ✳

Monster #1: Why did you gobble up
that physical trainer?
Monster #2: My mad doctor told me to
eat some healthy food.

✳ ✳ ✳

Son: Mom, the meatballs you made for
dinner are hard as rocks.
Mother: Humph! If you don't like them,
just throw them out the window.
Son: I did and hit a passerby on
the head. Now he's lying there
unconscious.

MENU NOTICE

**Try our fairy tale platter—
you can eat it with your
Hans-el and Gretel.**

Waiter: Will there be anything else, sir?
Customer: Yes. I'll have a side order of
spare ribs.

Barry: Do you want to hear a good joke
about bland food?
Harry: No thanks. I don't care for
tasteless humor.

53

Man: There are little rodents
   swimming in that pitcher of milk.
Farmer: That's not milk. It's mice
   cream.

Ed: You eat like a pig.
Fred: Your remark is a slop in my face.

Chester: I got fired from my job at the deli counter.

Lester: Why? Were you bad at slicing ham?

Chester: No. I was too good at cutting the cheese.

✳ ✳ ✳

Mother: Son, you can't eat my homemade soup with a fork.

Son: I'm not trying to eat the soup, Mom. I'm trying to spear a fly.

✳ ✳ ✳

Why does Godzilla eat garbage trucks?

He likes to snack on junk food.

What's the most revolting soup in the world?

Spit-pea soup.

✳ ✳ ✳

Mrs. Robin: We're having mud pies filled with earthworms for dessert.

Mr. Robin: Oh boy! Let's dig in!

✳ ✳ ✳

KNOCK! KNOCK!

Who's there?

Howdy.

Howdy who?

Howdy flies got in your stew I do not know.

Son: Ick! How do you expect me to eat liver and onions, Mom. It makes me sick just to look at and smell this meal.

Mother: Well, close your eyes, hold your nose, and open your mouth.

❋ ❋ ❋

Father: Finish your dinner. Fish is brain food.

Daughter: Anything that eats worms can't be very smart.

❋ ❋ ❋

What's black and white and purple all over?

A sloppy penguin who just drank a pitcher of grape juice.

TONGUE TWISTED

Surly Shirley surely swills sloppy Slappy's sappy syrup.

Waiter: This platter is our sanitation man special.

Customer: Who'd eat that garbage?

✹ ✹ ✹

Waiter: This platter is our acrobat special.

Customer: Just looking at it makes my stomach do flip-flops.

Big Al: What did you just serve me?
Waiter: You just ate some tripe, sir.
Big Al: What's tripe?
Waiter: It's ox intestine.
Big Al: It took a lot of guts to feed
me that.

Waiter: This platter is our talkative
   lawyer special.
Customer: It looks more like a gag
   order to me.

✻ ✻ ✻

Waiter: This platter is our teenagers'
   room special.
Customer: Who'd eat that mess?

✻ ✻ ✻

Customer: Hey! This roast duck still
   has some feathers on it.
Waiter: Stop complaining and chow
   down.

MENU NOTICE
Try our buffalo burger—
it's just plain meat.

Mr. Frog: Fireflies are my favorite food.
Mr. Toad: I like hot meals, too.

✳ ✳ ✳

Mr. Worm: Mr. and Mrs. Bluejay
invited me over for dinner tonight.
Mr. Bug: If I were you, I'd wiggle out of
that invitation any way I could.

Father: How long do you expect to keep a live lobster as a pet?
Son: Just until he gets into hot water.

✳ ✳ ✳

Kenny: The hot lunch at school today made me ill.
Jenny: Why didn't you return it?
Kenny: I did. I threw up all over the cafeteria.

Where does a pig farmer buy food for his hungry hogs?
    At a sloppin' mall.

✳ ✳ ✳

Sea Captain: Do you still keep Maryland Blue Crabs as pets?
Sailor: Nah! I got boiling mad at them last Saturday.

✳ ✳ ✳

Rudy: Do you want to share my last stick of gum?
Judy: That depends who gets to chew it first.

Father: Stop reaching across the table for the gravy. Don't you have a tongue?
Son: Yes, but my arms are longer.

✳ ✳ ✳

Customer: Waiter, bring me a steak and step on it.
Waiter: I'm sorry, sir. Stepping on food is a violation of the health code.

MENU NOTICE
Try our King Kong sandwich—you'll go ape over the taste.

Baby Bird: Ick! Are we having worm
   burgers for dinner again?
Mother Bird: Yes, why?
Baby Bird: It's disgusting! Why can't
   we have something normal for once?
Mother Bird: Like what?
Baby Bird: Like baked beetles or
   termite casserole.

DUMB LAST WORDS

"Hey! Don't bite my head off,"
said the rude waiter to the
impatient hungry lion.
Snap!

"The drinks are on me,"
said the Transylvanian bartender
to the thirsty vampires.
Slurp!

*"I dare you to eat me on
Thanksgiving,"* said the defiant
turkey to the starving Pilgrims.
Gobble gobble!

What soda do weirdos drink?
 Kook-a-cola.

✻ ✻ ✻

**What happened to the kid who
drank eight bottles of lemon soda?**
 He burped seven up.

✻ ✻ ✻

What is a frog's favorite soft drink?
 Croak-a-cola.

✻ ✻ ✻

Customer: Waiter, there's a fly in my
 soup.
Waiter: Don't worry, sir. The spider in
 your bread basket will get him.

Man: Last year your apples had worms in them. This year your pears have worms in them.

Farmer: Don't blame me. There was a bad apple crop this year so the worms are experiencing a housing shortage.

Why was Mr. Echo so upset?
He ate something that kept repeating on him.

✳ ✳ ✳

KNOCK! KNOCK!

Who's there?
I'm tofu.
I'm tofu who?
I'm tofu to eat any more of this slop.

✳ ✳ ✳

Mother: Why are you keeping a box of dirt in our kitchen?

Little Girl: That's not dirt. It's instant mud pie mix. All you have to do is add water.

What happened to the man who ate duck feathers?

He couldn't keep his meal down.

✻ ✻ ✻

What does a messy leatherneck soldier eat for lunch?

A slob marine sandwich.

✻ ✻ ✻

What dessert uses paste in its recipe?

Glue berry pie.

✻ ✻ ✻

What do unsophisticated mountain folk slurp tea from?

Hick-cups.

ATTENTION DINERS
Before you eat corn on the cob, be sure to always wash your ears.

What did the tough singer eat for lunch?

A gangsta wrap.

✳ ✳ ✳

Customer: Waiter, my salad is pitch black.

Waiter: That's not salad, sir, it's coal slaw.

71

HOW DO YOU WANT YOUR PIZZA?

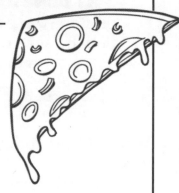

Mr. Aardvark—
"Topped with ant-chovies."

Mr. Podiatrist—
"Topped with peppers and bunions."

Mr. Newspaper Editor—
"Topped with 'Extra!' cheese."

Mr. Huskie—
"Topped with mush-rooms."

Mr. Snowplow—
"Topped with slush-rooms."

Ms. Cheerleader—
"Topped with pep-pep-pepper!"

Ms. Matchmaker—
"Topped with meet sauce."

Cougar: Why did you devour that pioneer?
Bear: I needed something to settle my upset stomach.

❋ ❋ ❋

Customer: Waiter, there's a bug on my ice cream cake.
Waiter: Relax, sir, it's fly à la mode.

❋ ❋ ❋

How do you make a ground meat pizza?

Drop a meat pizza face down on the ground, pick it up, and serve it.

Customer: Waiter, what are those icky
things wiggling around in my broth?
Waiter: It's what you ordered, sir.
Customer: I ordered warm soup.
Waiter: Excuse me, sir.
I thought you said
worm soup.

How do you make a cold cheese pizza?

Prepare a cheese pizza and then get a person with a bad cold to sneeze all over it.

✳ ✳ ✳

Lady: Ick! Eating ice cream out of your bare hand is unsanitary.

Boy: Well, it was either eat it this way or leave it on the ground where it fell.

✳ ✳ ✳

What do you get if you eat mud pies?

A filthy mouth.

TONGUE TWISTED

Hairy Harry Healey hurled
cheesy cheddar chunks chilly
Chester Chalmers churned.

Monster #1: Why did you devour that
  genius?
Monster #2: My mad doctor told me to
  eat smart from now on.

✳ ✳ ✳

What's red and bumpy and costs five
cents at a bakery?
  Pimple-nickel bread.

Jack: These snack pastries are making me burp.
Mack: Maybe they're hic-cupcakes.

✳ ✳ ✳

KNOCK! KNOCK!
Who's there?
Mister E.
Mister E who?
Mister E food is what we're having for lunch in school today.

✳ ✳ ✳

What do you get when you throw a cow into a blender?
A smoooothie.

Mrs. Aardvark: Today we're having ants for breakfast and ants for lunch.

Mr. Aardvark: What's for dinner?

Mrs. Aardvark: Fireflies. I thought we'd have a light supper for a change.

✳ ✳ ✳

Mother: Your bully cousin told me he spit on your hamburger at the family barbecue.

Little Boy: Yes, Mom. But don't worry. I didn't eat it.

Mother: That's good. What did you do with it?

Little Boy: I traded it to Grandpa for his hotdog.

What do you get when an icky bug falls into a cup of steamy chocolate?
A hot cocoa roach.

❉ ❉ ❉

Mother: Billy, don't use a spoon to scratch your back. It's wrong.
Billy: You're right, Mom. A fork will work much better.

❉ ❉ ❉

Girl: Yuk! Stop eating that. There are ants all over your vanilla ice cream.
Boy: Ha! Ha! Relax. Can't you tell chocolate sprinkles from ants?
Girl: Yes. The sprinkles are the black specks that aren't wiggling.

What do you get if you cross a turkey with an octopus?

Plenty of extra drumsticks on Thanksgiving.

✳ ✳ ✳

Teacher: Johnny, don't use that spoon to eat your lunch. I saw you drop it on the floor.

Johnny: It's okay, Teacher. I used my handkerchief to wipe it clean.

Teacher: Thank goodness you brought a handkerchief to school today.

Johnny: You're telling me. I've been blowing my runny nose in it all morning.

TONGUE TWISTED
Eager Eddie ate eight icky earthworms.

What did the waiter say to the pig farmer?

Will you be having swine with your dinner, sir?

* * *

Iggy: My sister thinks she's a picnic lunch.

Ziggy: She sounds like a basket case to me.

Customer: Waiter, there's a fly in my chili.

Waiter: I know sir. It's our flyday special.

* * *

Mother: Son, it's rude to slurp tomato soup from your spoon. Please stop it.

Son: Okay, Mom. Hand me a straw.

* * *

What's the difference between boogers, broccoli, and cauliflower?

Kids don't eat broccoli and cauliflower.

Why was sloppy Marco sad?
He spilled grape juice on his favorite polo shirt.

✳ ✳ ✳

What do Italian aardvarks eat?
Ant-d-pasta.

✳ ✳ ✳

Son: Our dog ate the take home test I had to complete this weekend.
Father: Don't worry. I'm sure he'll pass it before Monday morning.

KNOCK! KNOCK!
Who's there?
Stan.
Stan who?
Stan back! I'm
gonna hurl!

Man: Waiter, there's a golf ball in my pasta.

Waiter: It only looks like a golf ball, sir. It's really a meatball. It comes with our nine course meal.

SICK DINNER SIGN
All you can eat chili served here. Stop in and fill up on gas.

KNOCK! KNOCK!
Who's there?
Enos.
Enos who?
Enos who puked in the boys' locker room.

✳ ✳ ✳

How did the atomic submarine sink to the bottom of the ocean?
The cook served chili with beans to the crew and the captain opened a window to let in fresh air.

✳ ✳ ✳

Customer: Why is there a feather in my salmon?
Waiter: That's our tickled pink salmon dinner, sir.

KNOCK! KNOCK!

Who's there?

Theresa.

Theresa who?

Theresa big ugly bug in my soup.

❊ ❊ ❊

Bully: How'd you like a knuckle sandwich?

Boy: No thanks. I promised my mom I'd stop eating fist food.

SOMETHING SMELLS FUNNY

KNOCK! KNOCK!
Who's there?
Pool.
Pool who?
Pool my finger, dude!

✳ ✳ ✳

Which armored vehicle smells the worst?
The septic tank.

White House Aide #1: Cancel the press conference. The president has a bad case of stomach gas.

White House Aide #2: Gosh! I hope the news reporters don't get wind of this story!

✻ ✻ ✻

What do you get if you cross a flying nocturnal creature with a skunk?
A bat odor.

✻ ✻ ✻

Marty: Your car smells awful.

Artie: That's because the engine has gas problems.

What's the best thing to do if King Kong eats two tons of chili beans?
Hold your nose and run for the hills!

✳ ✳ ✳

Tim: That tornado smells bad.
Jim: It's just a whirl wind.

SMELLY SIGN OF THE TIMES
Acme Sewer Company—
we keep everyone's business
running smoothly.

What did General Skunk say to his stinky soldiers before the big battle?

Men, the smell of victory is in the air.

Who invented skunk cell phones?

Alexander Graham Smell.

What do you call a skunk who disagrees with everyone?

A dis-scenter.

Why was the skunk author so proud?

His new book was number one on the Best Smeller List.

Mrs. Skunk to Mr. Skunk: "I feel like having Italian food tonight. Please odor us a pizza."

Why did the skunk powder his body with sugar?
He wanted to smell sweet.

What happens if you hang upside down for too long?

Your nose runs and your feet smell.

❇ ❇ ❇

What do you get when you feed chili beans to a math teacher?

Gas problems.

FOUL CRIME

Number Two arrested Number Three for attacking a fellow number with a knife. The charge was that Number Three cut one.

What is S.M.E.L. 108.2 on your radio dial?

It's the gas station.

❋ ❋ ❋

How can you tell if your sports coach thinks you stink?

He thinks you stink if he hands you a uniform and says you're number two.

❋ ❋ ❋

Bill: I have a pet skunk who likes to eat onions and garlic.

Will: I bet you can smell him coming and going.

KNOCK! KNOCK!

Who's there?

Harry.

Harry who?

Harry armpits.

✳ ✳ ✳

Matt: Our family car runs on baked beans, chili beans, and pinto beans.

Pat: Does it get good gas mileage?

Matt: Yes, but it backfires a lot.

✳ ✳ ✳

What did Captain Smelly say to Sergeant Skunk?

Sergeant, you have your marching odors.

What did the owl say when it flew into the Limburger factory?

Who? Who? Who cut the cheese?

✳ ✳ ✳

KNOCK! KNOCK!

Who's there?

Stan Key.

Stan Key who?

Stan Key diapers. P.U.!

97

Beth: I smell a flock of sheep.
Seth: Is it a baa odor?

What do you call a comic book hero who cleans up after his pet dog?

A super dooper pooper scooper upper.

TONGUE TWISTED

Six slick sick sailors saw
seven swift short ships
sailing south.

What did the rooster say when he saw dog poop?

Cock-a-doodle-doo-doo!

* * *

Jack: How do you like delivering propane gas?

Mack: Frankly, my job stinks.

KNOCK! KNOCK!

Who's there?

Wendy.

Wendy who?

Wendy toilet starts to overflow, use the plunger.

❄ ❄ ❄

Where does a sea dog do his business?

On the ship's poop deck.

❄ ❄ ❄

Boy: Don't be afraid of my pet skunk. The vet fixed him so he doesn't smell bad anymore.

Man: In that case, you should hang an OUT OF ODOR sign on him.

Which bird is always in the bathroom?

The stool pigeon.

✳ ✳ ✳

Millie: My father is a real comedian. My mom loves to clown around. My brother is a practical joker. Living at my place is a million laughs.

Tillie: Now I understand why your house always smells funny.

✳ ✳ ✳

Student: Teacher, is my breath really bad?

Teacher: Ugh! Please keep your mouth closed until the bell rings.

What patriotic song really stinks?
Yankee Doo Doo Dandy.

TONGUE TWISTED
**Five hearty fools
fight Hugh Pugh.**

Beth: I smell chickens.
Seth: Is it a fowl odor?

KNOCK! KNOCK!

Who's there?

Sire Lint.

Sire Lint who?

Sire Lint but deadly.

❋ ❋ ❋

Sailor: Why do these playing cards smell so bad?

Mate: I guess it's a poop deck.

❋ ❋ ❋

What is one base a baseball player never wants to step on?

Turd base.

What comes near the middle of a baseball game and smells awful?

The seventh inning stench.

* * *

Which baby felines have a lot of stomach problems?

Gas-kits.

* * *

KNOCK! KNOCK!

Who's there?

Kenya.

Kenya who?

Kenya wait until I go to the bathroom?

Penny: Thanks for inviting me over to
your house to see your pet.
Jenny: You're welcome. Come on in.
Penny: Phew! It smells like your cat's
litter box needs to be changed.
Jenny: Humph! How dare you insult
me like that. The only pet I have is a
goldfish!

FOUL SMELLING PHILOSOPHY

When you're driving down life's highway and your vehicle is low on fuel, try not to pass any gas.

Student: Teacher! Teacher! Tell me the truth. Do my armpits smell?

Teacher: Ugh! I won't answer that, but please, please put your arm down.

Which friend of Peter Pan smells awful?
Stinkerbelle.

* * *

What kind of sneeze smells bad?
Limburger sneeze.

* * *

What do you call a smelly mutant superhero?
X-stinked.

* * *

Nellie: Why does this peach orchard stink so bad?
Shelly: The fruit must have smelly pits.

Circus Clown: Oh my gosh! What a
terrible noise! Was that thunder?
Animal Trainer: No. One of the
elephants has stomach gas.

What do you call dumb doody?
Nincompoop.

**Which famous western marshall had
stomach gas?**
Wyatt Burp.

Fred: The cost of underarm deodorant is going up.

Jed: I smell a price fixing scheme.

KNOCK! KNOCK!

Who's there?

Norway.

Norway who?

Norway, dude. I'm not using the bathroom until you let in some fresh air!

GAG ON THESE

What did one pimple say to the other?

You're my main squeeze.

* * *

What goes "Whew! Drip! Drip! Drip! Whew!"?

A sick snowman with a high fever.

What happened to the farmer who crossed clocks with rabbits?

He got ticks in his hares.

* * *

What did the depressed mole say to the gopher?

I'm sick and tired of this hole thing.

* * *

Where does a blackbird put its dirty socks?

In a crow's hamper.

KNOCK! KNOCK!

Who's there?
Slum folks.
Slum folks who?
Slum folks like spinach. I don't.

✳ ✳ ✳

What did Dr. Jelly say to the sick jam?
Don't spread germs.

Girl: What's that icky thing?
Boy: It's booger pizza. Pick a slice.

✳ ✳ ✳

KNOCK! KNOCK!
Who's there?
Billie.
Billie who?
Billie aches are no fun.

✳ ✳ ✳

**What do
you call
a toothless,
buzzing insect?**
Gum Bee.

KNOCK! KNOCK!
Who's there?
Maya.
Maya who?
Maya please go to the bathroom now?

* * *

Jim: Does it cost a lot to use a pay toilet?
Tim: No. You just have to pay the going rate.

* * *

Why was Mrs. Kangaroo so upset in the morning?

Her little Joey wet his bed the night before.

Who is the world's smartest pig?
Professor Einswine.

✳ ✳ ✳

Larry: Did you read the story about the kangaroo with broken legs who could never jump again?
Cary: No, but I bet it had an unhoppy ending.

✳ ✳ ✳

Student: I was playing my miniature harmonica and swallowed it.
Music Teacher: Quick! Take a note to the school nurse!

SICK SIGN
Acme Diaper Company—
we want to change the world.

**What do you get if you cross a
crocodile with a field of corn?**

A croc-of-crop.

✳ ✳ ✳

**When do book club members usually
have bowel movements?**

After readers digest.

117

Bert: Last night I stepped on a firefly
and squashed it flat.
Ernie: Now that's a blinkin' shame.

NOTICE
Little Bruce Wayne uses the
boys batroom at school.

KNOCK! KNOCK!
Who's there?
Ivan.
Ivan who?
Ivan throwing up all day.

TONGUE TWISTED
Pretty polished pine pooh pews.

KNOCK! KNOCK!
Who's there?
D.K.
D.K. who?
D.K. is the enemy of healthy teeth.

* * *

What do you get when you put a cow in a sauna?
Evaporated milk.

Which dinosaur had a lot of stomach gas?

The burpasaurus.

Which cow is always full of garbage?

The dump-steer.

**What do you get if you cross
a singing lesson with an army
bathroom?**

A la-la-la-la-la-latrine!

✳ ✳ ✳

**What do you call throwing up after
going on an amusement park ride?**

Wheegurgitation.

SICK SIGN
Ace Bathroom Company—
we stall our customers.

Mr. Mosquito: There's a new bug
zapper in the back yard.
Ms. Moth: That's shocking news!

❋ ❋ ❋

KNOCK! KNOCK!
Who's there?
Ty Ann.
Ty Ann who?
Ty Ann go before we leave on our road
trip.

❋ ❋ ❋

Joe: What do you get if you cross
racehorses with dinosaurs?
Moe: I don't know, but I'm not shoveling
out that stable.

KNOCK! KNOCK!

Who's there?

Paul.

Paul who?

Paul over at the next rest stop.

❊ ❊ ❊

How do you make a tissue dance?

Put a little boogie in it.

❊ ❊ ❊

Sergeant: I'm sorry, General. You can't use that restroom.

General: Why not?

Sergeant: It's a private bathroom.

123

What smells and is wooly?
A compost sheep.

* * *

What do you call a surfer who picks his nose?
A boogie boarder.

* * *

Why can't you keep a convict with acne in jail?
Because he's always breaking out.

* * *

What do you call Attila when he's all dirty?
Hun sanitary.

What do you get if Dracula bites Attila on the neck?

The Hun Dead.

✳ ✳ ✳

What do you get if you cross a buccaneer with a cow that's very ill?

Pirated moo sick.

✳ ✳ ✳

What do you call a baby chicken in a bathroom?

Toilet peeper.

✳ ✳ ✳

Abe: What's wrong with Mr. Van Winkle's pants?

Lincoln: They have a rip in them.

What do you call a nuclear powered messy leatherneck soldier?

An atomic slob marine.

TONGUE TWISTED

Gritty green grass gives giddy
Gussie Goose gross gas.

What did the surfer bug say to the mosquito?

Hey, dude! You suck!

What did the bathroom sink say to the sick toilet?

You look a bit flushed.

✳ ✳ ✳

Mr. Tuna: How's your life?
Mr. Shark: It bites.

GROSS PUPPET GAGS

Detective: I have proof that Pinocchio is guilty of the crime.
D.A.: Let's nail him.

✳ ✳ ✳

Jiminy: Ouch! I'm never shaking hands with you again, Pinocchio.
Pinocchio: Why not? Did I squeeze too hard?
Jiminy: No. You gave me a splinter.

✳ ✳ ✳

Pinocchio: Every time I tell a lie, my nose gets bigger.
Jiminy: Well, either start telling the truth or go see a cosmetic surgeon.

MORE GROSS PUPPET GAGS

Where does Pinocchio buy his spare parts?

At a chopping mall.

✳ ✳ ✳

What caused the untimely cremation of Pinocchio?

Gepetto ran out of firewood on a cold night.

✳ ✳ ✳

What do you find in Pinocchio's wooden ears?

Furniture wax.

What does Pinocchio have nightmares about?

Woodpeckers, termites, chain saws, and wood chippers.

ATTENTION
Pinocchio is pretty smart for a guy who started out as a blockhead!

EVEN MORE GROSS PUPPET GAGS

Jiminy: Does Pinocchio wear cotton underwear?
Cricket: No. He wears wooden drawers.

✳ ✳ ✳

Pinocchio doesn't grow, he just sprouts up.

✳ ✳ ✳

Pinocchio snacks on wood chips.

✳ ✳ ✳

Pinocchio's mom works at a bank. She's a branch manager.

Pinocchio went on a T.V. quiz show and got stumped.

✳ ✳ ✳

Pinocchio's family tree is full of saps.

✳ ✳ ✳

Pinocchio's pet elephant has a tree trunk.

What's the worst practical joke you can play on Pinocchio?
Give him a hot foot.

✳ ✳ ✳

What did Pinocchio have for dinner?
A wooden steak.

Mr. Green: Last summer our pet Great Dane ruined our back yard barbecue.

Mr. White: How did he do that?

Mr. Green: Let's just say he was a real party pooper.

✳ ✳ ✳

What did one pimply baseball player shout to the other?
Yo!
Heads up!

135

SICK DEFINITION
Sit-up instructor—
a human waist expert.

A hungry frog and toad were visiting by a pond and snacking on bugs. After a while the toad said, "It's time to go home to our lake."

"Already?" sighed the frog sadly. "Gee, time sure is fun when you're having flies."

Doctor: You have appendicitis.
Patient: You're kidding me. Right, Doc?
Doctor: No, I'm not.
Patient: Ah, cut it out already.

✳ ✳ ✳

David: I knew a sheep herder who made his rams wear crash helmets.
Joshua: Why did he do that?
David: He wanted them to protect their butts.

✳ ✳ ✳

Neighbor: Does your new puppy do his business outside?
Boy: Yes. During the week he takes quite a few business trips.

SICK QUESTION
Do poultry farmers
have fowl breath?

KNOCK! KNOCK!
Who's there?

Amos.

Amos who?

Amos stop picking my nose.

✳ ✳ ✳

Pirate: What's causing my hearing loss,
Doctor?

Doctor: Buccaneer wax.

Kindergarten Teacher: Today we're going to learn how to count from one to ten.

Pupil: Stop after you get to five, Teacher, so I can leave the room.

Kindergarten Teacher: Why do you have to leave the room?

Pupil: My parents are against six education in public school.

Al: I got a ticket for walking my dog in the park.

Hal: Was he on a leash?

Al: Yes.

Hal: Then why did you get a ticket?

Al: I walked my dog past a park bench with a sign on it. The sign read, "Wet paint," so that's just what my dog did.

Customer: Yuk! This salad is awful!
  Were these vegetables washed?
Waiter: Of course they were, sir. Look
  closely. There's still soap on them.

❋ ❋ ❋

**Who threw up during a famous
Roman chariot race?**
  Ben Hurl.

❋ ❋ ❋

**Which bathroom does the president
use when he's in Washington, D.C.?**
  It depends. Sometimes he uses the
Democratic potty and sometimes he
uses the Republican potty.

What fairy tale skunk wears glass slippers?

Scenterella.

❄ ❄ ❄

What's dumber than looking up when a flock of migrating birds is flying over?

Looking up with your mouth open.

SICK QUESTION
Do babies who live on farms soil their diapers?

What's worse than an elephant with stomach gas?

A hippo with diarrhea.

What do you find beneath the toes of stampeding elephants?

People who run too slow.

Why was Peter afraid to swim in the Neverland Ocean?

He saw a pan-eating shark in the water.

Mr. Fridge: Phew! This kitchen smells bad.

Mr. Sink: Don't look at me, pal. The stove has gas.

Clem: Where do all the bugs go in
   winter?
Zeke: Search me.
Clem: No thanks. I'm not that curious.

✳ ✳ ✳

**What did the sheriff say to the
outlaws who didn't use deodorant?**
   Get your hands up! Phew! Quick! Put
them down.

✳ ✳ ✳

Ms. Moth: Ick! Why is your hair so
   sticky?
Ms. Bee: I used a honey comb.

Grandfather: Have you ever used bug spray before?

Little Boy: No. Why would I want to spray bugs on myself?

SICK, SICK SNICKERS

How did author Charlotte Brontë keep her house smelling so nice?

She used lots of Jane Eyre freshener.

✳ ✳ ✳

What do you call a bathroom for young men in Scotland?

The Laddy's room.

What do you get if you cross an acrobat with toilet paper?

Something that can do great forward rolls and backward rolls.

✳ ✳ ✳

Bird #1: I want to eat some beetles.
Bird #2: So do I. Let's go out to crunch.

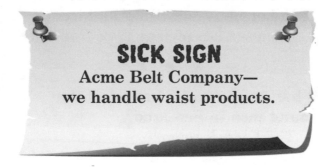

SICK SIGN
Acme Belt Company—
we handle waist products.

What does a racecar driver get if he eats spicy food?

Indy-gestion.

✳ ✳ ✳

How was the ear of corn born?

The stalk brought him.

✳ ✳ ✳

What has superpowers and gets walked on?

The Fantastic Floor.

✳ ✳ ✳

What weighs 800 pounds and has a hairy body and a shiny head?

A prematurely bald gorilla.

What do you find in a mutt's ear?
Cur wax.

❋ ❋ ❋

What do you get if you give a rabbit a perm?
Curly hare.

❋ ❋ ❋

What sleeps for twenty years and has ripples?
Rip Van Crinkle.

❋ ❋ ❋

Lester: I wrote a sloppy sentence and put a gross period at the end of it.
Chester: Dot's disgusting.

How did the pear get a bruise?
Fruit punch.

* * *

What did the sneaker say to the nasty shoe?
Quit sticking your tongue out at me.

* * *

Why did Gretel get rid of the family dog?
Because it bit the Hans-el that fed it.

* * *

Big Al: Can a police detective fry a chicken?
Big Sal: No. But he can grill a canary.

151

What did the laxative say to the digestive system?

Don't mind me, I'm just passing through.

❋ ❋ ❋

What do you get if you cross a salmon with a moron?

A fish that doesn't know if it should swim upstream or downstream to spawn.

TONGUE TWISTED
See Sally Shore sell smelly seashells.

What brand of underwear does a goony bird wear?

Fruit of the Loon.

What did the neat Sasquatch spend all of his money on?

Hair gel.

What's black and white and blue in the face?

A spoiled penguin holding its breath.

✳ ✳ ✳

What was wrong with the sick clam?

It had mussel cramps.

✳ ✳ ✳

What do you get if you cross a hen with static electricity?

Chicken à la cling.

✳ ✳ ✳

What sloppy creature lives in Scotland?

The Loch Mess Monster.

Son: I'm starved. What's cooking?
Mother: We're having kangaroo steaks
   tonight.
Son: On second thought, I'll just skip
   dinner.

✳ ✳ ✳

**What cartoon bird uses foul
language and always has to be
censored?**
   Bleep! Bleep! The Roadrunner.

✳ ✳ ✳

Can a desert throw up?
   No. It gets the dry heaves.

KNOCK! KNOCK!
Who's there?

Musk.
Musk who?

Musk you always be so sloppy?

✳ ✳ ✳

What's black and white and red all over?

A penguin with a bad nose bleed.

✳ ✳ ✳

What did Bugs Bunny say to the geek?

What's up, dork?

Why did the pigs go to the casino?
They wanted to play the slop machines.

* * *

What did the needle say to the thread?
Hey! Quit poking me in the eye.

* * *

Who sells sloppy ice cream?
The Goo Humor Man.

* * *

Why did Mrs. Doe scold her baby son?
Because he kept running around the house buck naked.

Which soft drink smells like sewage?
Poopsie-cola.

✳ ✳ ✳

Why did the comedian wear goofy jockey shorts?
Because they were funderwear.

✳ ✳ ✳

How do you make grasshopper soup?
Boil some spring water and then throw in the bugs.

GROSS MONSTER GIGGLERS

What kind of stomach problems did Dracula have?

He suffered from supernatural gas.

* * *

What do you get when Sasquatch jumps in front of a speeding train?

Sasquish!

* * *

How do you cook scrambled dinosaur eggs?

First melt a ton of butter in the world's biggest frying pan.

What does Godzilla do after he goes to the bathroom?

He flushes Tokyo Bay.

* * *

Why did the skeleton army lose every battle?

None of its soldiers had any guts.

TEACHER TO CLASS

I'm going to tell you a Greek myth about flying monsters that has a harpy ending.

How can skeletons afford to go to college?

They get skullerships.

✳ ✳ ✳

What does Dracula use at a bus stop?

The public batroom.

✳ ✳ ✳

What buzzes, lives in hives, and attacks Scotsmen?

Kilter bees.

✳ ✳ ✳

Why doesn't the Invisible Man have acne problems?

He has a clear complexion.

What is Beethoven doing in his grave?

Decomposing.

✳ ✳ ✳

What do Egyptians listen to while making mummies?

Wrap music.

✳ ✳ ✳

How do you keep a mummy smelling fresh?

Use plastic wrap.

163

Why did the dragon devour Sir Lancelot when he was tardy for their appointment?

Because he felt like having a late knight snack.

❋ ❋ ❋

What do you get if you cross Dr. Frankenstein with his monster?

A self-made man.

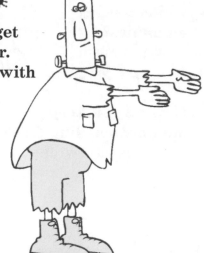

What do you get if you cross a prehistoric cat with a male deer?

A saber-toothed tiger with buck teeth.

* * *

How do you kill a fish that's been bitten by a vampire?

You put a juicy worm on a silver hook.

* * *

What do you call a wrestling match between werewolves?

A fur brawl.

* * *

What weighs a ton and hops?

One of King Kong's fleas.

165

What's fifty stories high, has huge horns, and butts its head against skyscrapers?

Goatzilla.

❊ ❊ ❊

What do you get if you cross Godzilla with your pet cat?

The biggest litter box you can find.

❊ ❊ ❊

What do you get if you cross a dinosaur with a pigeon?

I don't know, but look out below if it has to go.

NOTICE
Count Dracula has
bat breath.

Monster: I was so sick last night I
puked my guts out.
Skeleton: That's one problem I never
have.

❋ ❋ ❋

**What did the werewolf say to the
cheese salesman?**
I'll tear you limb from Limburger.

Dr. Frankenstein: Why were you afraid to tell me I left a big hole where your stomach should be?

Monster: No guts, I guess.

✳ ✳ ✳

Monster: Dr. Frankenstein, can you give me a hand here?

Dr. Frankenstein: Right or left?

✳ ✳ ✳

Igor: Why is your monster hopping around and eating carrots?

Mad Doctor: It's one of my hare-brained experiments.

NOTICE
Undertakers are like pet
cats. They both do their
business and then bury it.

Creature:
Doc, I
want to stay
a really dumb
monster.
Mad Doctor: Well stop
bothering me before I
brain you.

Igor: Why didn't you finish giving your monster artificial life?

Mad Doctor: I didn't have the heart to finish the job.

NOTICE
A mummy is never the life of a Halloween party.

Why doesn't the Frankenstein Monster go to football games?

He gets so excited he yells his head off.

170

Monster: Dr. Frankenstein, you forgot to stitch up my abdomen.

Dr. Frankenstein: Well, don't spill your guts to me about it.

❋ ❋ ❋

Monster: Dr. Frankenstein, you sewed my arms on backwards.

Dr. Frankenstein: Well, pat yourself on your back for noticing my mistake.

❋ ❋ ❋

Monster: Dr. Frankenstein, why did you give me the brain of a rabbit?

Dr. Frankenstein: Because I want you to think hoppy thoughts.

Monster: Dr. Frankenstein, you gave me two left feet.

Dr. Frankenstein: So what, you're a monster not a dancer.

✳ ✳ ✳

Why did the mummy wet himself?
He couldn't get undressed fast enough.

NOTICE
Werewolves and vampires
have jobs that bite.

What happened to the bunch of grapes who revolted and refused to be turned into juice?

They suffered a crushing defeat.

✳ ✳ ✳

Ken: Don't let my dog lick your face.
Len: Why not?
Ken: Haven't you ever heard of barkteria?

✳ ✳ ✳

Corporal Van: This is my filthy bathroom. This is my sloppy room. This is my untidy closet.
Captain Dan: What's that, sir?
Corporal Van: That's my mess hall.

What kind of ointment does a skunk use on his sore muscles?
Stink balm.

SICK SHOUT OUT
Knight: Hey Mr. Dragon! Use some mouthwash. Your breath isn't so hot.

Mr. Beetle: Where is Mr. Firefly?
Mr. Ant: He flew off into the darkness.
Mr. Beetle: Oh well, when you gotta glow you gotta glow.

Barry: My friend Jake picks his feet.
My friend Buster picks his nose. My
friend Pete picks his ear. Would you
like to meet them?
Larry: No, thanks. Your friends are too
picky for me.

❋ ❋ ❋

**What's made out of wood, has a
quarter moon on the front door,
and is taller than the Empire State
Building?**
Paul Bunyon's outhouse.

❋ ❋ ❋

**What does Pinocchio get if he
swallows a lit match?**
Severe heartburn.

What do you call a dried-up cow?
A milk dud.

✳ ✳ ✳

What makes Robin the Boy Wonder laugh out loud?
Batroom humor.

✳ ✳ ✳

KNOCK! KNOCK!
Who's there?
Wilma.
Wilma who?
Wilma nose ever stop running?

✳ ✳ ✳

What kind of hens are always itchy?
Flea range chickens.

Why did the toddler rip the scab off of his cut?

He was playing peek a boo boo.

* * *

KNOCK! KNOCK!

Who's there?

Oscar.

Oscar who?

Oscar if she knows where the girls' room is.

* * *

Tall Paul: Did you tell the Green Giant he could have a lima bean?

Big Al: No. But I told him he could take a pea.

KNOCK! KNOCK!

Who's there?

Wheelbarrow.

Wheelbarrow who?

Wheelbarrow some tissues from the teacher to blow our noses.

* * *

Cary: Why are you staring into the mirror and keeping one eye closed?

Mary: This way my new hairstyle doesn't look half bad.

* * *

What does a comedian do before he takes a shower?

The comic strips.

Why are worms unsanitary?
Their homes are always dirty.

**How can you tell
if an elephant is
a salesman?**
If he's a salesman, he'll have
a sample case instead of a
trunk.

KNOCK! KNOCK!
Who's there?
Marcella.
Marcella who?
Marcella is so damp, mold is growing
everywhere.

179

KNOCK! KNOCK!

Who's there?

I'm Gladys.

I'm Gladys who?

I'm Gladys not me who smells bad.

✳ ✳ ✳

What's worse than a dumb comet?

A stupid asteroid.

TONGUE TWISTED

Slick Chick Duck upchucked
Cris Cluck's creamed corn.

Father: Who gave you that bloody nose?
Son: Nobody gave it to me. I had to
    fight for it.

* * *

KNOCK! KNOCK!

Who's there?
Harold.
Harold who?
Harold do you have to be to start using
deodorant?

* * *

Rob: I can't think straight in this cold,
    frigid weather.
Bob: I always knew you were a brrr
    brained guy.

GROSS FAREWELLS

What happened to the really old centipede?

He kicked, kicked, kicked, kicked off.

✳ ✳ ✳

What happened to the really old artist?

He drew his last breath.

✳ ✳ ✳

What happened to the really old NASCAR driver?

He went fast.

What happened to the really old real estate agent?

She bought the farm.

✳ ✳ ✳

What happened to the really old poker player?

He cashed in.

✳ ✳ ✳

What happened to the really old watchmaker?

His time ran out.

✳ ✳ ✳

What happened to the really old electrician?

Someone pulled the plug on him.

What happened to the really old motel clerk?

He checked out.

* * *

What happened to the really old video game designer?

It's game over.

* * *

What happened to the really old reporter?

I'm sorry to say the news is bad.

* * *

What happened to the really old quarterback?

He passed away.

What happened to the really old writer?

They closed the book on him.

* * *

What happened to the really old bus driver?

It was the end of the road.

* * *

What happened to the really old fried egg?

It was over easy.

SICK QUESTION
Do bathrooms in motor
homes have toilet seat belts?

KNOCK! KNOCK!
Who's there?
Izzy.
Izzy who?
Izzy gonna barf again?

187

KNOCK! KNOCK!

Who's there?

Kenny.

Kenny who?

Kenny slow down. I'm getting carsick.

* * *

KNOCK! KNOCK!

Who's there?

Hannah.

Hannah who?

Hannah 'nother thing: you need to use a stronger mouthwash.

RAUNCHY RIDDLERS

What did one piece of firewood say to the other?

Don't play with matches or you'll make an ash of yourself.

✳ ✳ ✳

What do you call a man who wrestles a hungry crocodile with only his right arm?

Lefty.

How do you pay for a booger?
You pay through the nose.

✳ ✳ ✳

What do you get if you cover a turtle with duck feathers?
Slow down.

✳ ✳ ✳

What do you get if you cross a woodpecker with a chicken?
A yellow-bellied sap clucker.

✳ ✳ ✳

Which football player is always running to the bathroom?
The piddle linebacker.

Who lives in Neverland and spends too much time in the bathroom?
Tinklebelle.

✳ ✳ ✳

What is a urologist's favorite fairy tale?
The Princess and the Pee.

✳ ✳ ✳

What is a urologist's favorite cartoon strip?
Peanuts.

✳ ✳ ✳

What's black and white and has a green face?
A seasick zebra.

KNOCK! KNOCK!

Who's there?

I. Burma.

I. Burma who?

I. Burma butt when I sat on a hot radiator.

SICK DEFINITION

Stomach crunches—
the regulation of human waist.

Ted: How did your dog get a bloody nose?

Fred: He chased a parked car.

Which creatures have the most stomach problems?

Gas-tropods.

* * *

What grows in a vegetable garden and fights crime?

Beetman.

* * *

What job does Bruce Wayne hate the most?

Cleaning the batroom bowl.

* * *

Nick: My vehicle doesn't backfire. It belches fumes.

Rick: Maybe it's a hiccup truck.

What's brown, has raisins for eyes, and runs around holding its side?

A gingerbread man with appendicitis.

✳ ✳ ✳

KNOCK! KNOCK!

Who's there?

M.T.

M.T. who?

M.T. the septic tank.

✳ ✳ ✳

What did the pea pods shout to the fertilizer at the football game?

We're number one. You're number two!

NOTICE
Farmers who sit down to
rest in muddy fields may soil
their pants.

What do you get if you cross a radio with onions and garlic?

Stations that broadcast bad breath.

Which person in Mother Goose Land lives on a garbage heap?

Humpty Dumpster.

Sadie: My boa constrictor likes you.
   Will you go out on a date with him?
Katie: Absolutely not! I don't want him
   to get a crush on me.

✵ ✵ ✵

Park Ranger: I
   know a grizzly
   who is so old
   he has no
   teeth. Now he's
   a real gummy
   bear.

✵ ✵ ✵

**What's red and white and freezing
cold?**
   A snowman with an acne problem.

Dell: Can hippos fly?
Mel: Yes. But only if they have a pilot's
   license.

✳ ✳ ✳

Zack: Can elephants fly?
Mack: Yes. But only if they have plane
   tickets.

✳ ✳ ✳

**What do you get from a vampire
snowman?**
   Frost bite.

✳ ✳ ✳

How did the shepherd get so dumb?
   The flock bleet his brains out.

197

Penguin #1: Your igloo is as filthy as a sty.

Penguin #2: I like to think of it as a pigloo.

❋ ❋ ❋

KNOCK! KNOCK!
Who's there?
Hutch.
Hutch who?
Stop sneezing all over me!

❋ ❋ ❋

What do you say when an Englishman moons someone?
London britches falling down.

Spud and Dudley were two country dogs who came to the city for the first time. As they walked down a street, Spud started to sniff around a fire hydrant. Meanwhile, Dudley stumbled onto a parking meter.

"What's this?" Dudley asked Spud.

"I'm not sure," Spud answered. "It looks like a pay toilet."

Who painted an abstract picture of a hog farmer?

Pigasso.

GROSS DEFINITION

Gut feeling– stomach guess.

Which American pioneer had really bad stomach gas?

Daniel Boom Boom.

Which football player is a butt head?
The hind end.

✳ ✳ ✳

Abe: Why is that sheep scratching so
much?
Dave: Its woolen underwear must itch.

✳ ✳ ✳

KNOCK! KNOCK!
Who's there?
Breed.
Breed who?
Breed through your mouth if your nose
is clogged up.

RAUNCHY BUSINESS CARDS

I.M. Regular–*Bran flakes salesman*

Andy Towelover–*Washroom attendant*

E.Z. Goin–*Prune juice maker*

Noah Clogs–*Sewer inspector*

M.T. Stalls–*Commercial bathroom repairman*

Lil Johns–*Acme Potty Company*

Piper Tissue–*Washroom accessories*

NASTY NEWS

Story: Killer clock convicted of murder and sentenced to the electric chair.
Headline–Time Fries.

Jack: I know two acrobats who can juggle a live turkey.

Mack: What do they do, flip each other the bird?

✳ ✳ ✳

Where does a small male ghost go to relieve himself?

He goes to the little boos room.

What did the withering tree say to the gardener?
Blight me!

* * *

Father: Junior, get out of the car and use the bathroom before we leave on our trip.
Son: No. And you can't make me go.

GROSS NOTICE
People who gives speeches on soil conservation talk dirty.

Sheriff: How did you learn about the outlaws we hanged?
Deputy: I heard a noose report.

＊　＊　＊

What's the worst exercise a male dog can do inside the house?
　　Leg lifts.

＊　＊　＊

　　Show me a snake on trial for assault . . . and I'll show you a defendant who doesn't have a leg to stand on.

＊　＊　＊

What does a Scotsman call a very tiny notebook?
　　A wee wee pad.

KNOCK! KNOCK!

Who's there?

Hal.

Hal who?

Hal vomit if I eat any more garlic bread.

❈ ❈ ❈

Author: I wrote a play called "Life Is a Pig Sty."

Producer: Do me a favor and clean up your acts.

❈ ❈ ❈

What do you call an athlete covered in a thin layer of ice?

Jock Frost.

What does Mr. Paste use in order to smell nice?

Stick deodorant.

GROSS NOTICE
Athletic people with very
long legs usually have nice
high-knees.

What do sailors use in order to smell nice?

Row-on deodorant.

Mother: How was the party?
Son: After I ate dessert I couldn't stop belching.
Mother: I warned you not to eat too much burpday cake.

✳ ✳ ✳

What's more gross than a hippo picking its teeth?

An elephant picking its nose.

✳ ✳ ✳

What did one dog say to the other who was sniffing around the fire hydrant?

Hey, pal! Keep your nose out of my business.

**What's green and
grows in sewer
pipes?**
Sewage
plants.

✳ ✳ ✳

**How can you
tell a messy tree from a neat tree?**
A messy tree will have piggy bark.

GROSS NEWS FLASH
Golfers often use
fore letter words.

209

What did Mr. Cigar say to the Cigarette Brothers?

Pull up your pants, boys! Your butts are showing.

* * *

Why did the flea jump off of the short dog and hop onto the tall pig?

It wanted to live high on the hog for a while.

* * *

Customer: I'll have the turtle soup.

Waiter: We have a special today on split pea soup, sir.

Customer: Okay. Hold the turtle and make it pea.

210

What's worse than a brook that babbles on?

A river with a big mouth.

＊ ＊ ＊

What lies at the bottom of the ocean and twitches?

A nervous wreck.

＊ ＊ ＊

What do you serve a detective for dessert?

A cop cake.

＊ ＊ ＊

What's white, lives in the snow, and has uncontrollable mood swings?

A bi-polar bear.

Joe: I crossed a centipede with Smokey the Bear.

Moe: What did you get?

Joe: I'm not sure, but it's great at stamping out forest fires.

❋ ❋ ❋

Zack: Has anyone ever given you a wedgie?

Mack: Yes. I've been the butt of that stupid practical joke.

❋ ❋ ❋

Farley: I carve skunks out of wood.

Charley: You're just a whittle stinker, aren't you.

YUK! SICKENING WORDS OF LOVE

Mr. Realtor–
You mean a lot to me.

Mr. Musician–
When I see you, my heart skips a beat.

Mr. Coal Worker–
Please say you'll be mine.

Mr. Coin Dealer–
Our love is mint to be.

Mr. Sailor–
I only have aye-ayes for you.

KNOCK! KNOCK!

Who's there?

Anita.

Anita who?

Anita bath very badly.

Mr. Snotty: Please don't bring your cat into my house. It's full of fleas.

Mr. Cootie: In that case you should call an exterminator.

✳ ✳ ✳

Clara: Is that pig wearing blue pants?

Sara: Yes. Haven't you ever seen pork in jeans before?

✳ ✳ ✳

Parasite #1: Where did you go to college?

Parasite #2: Georgia Tick.

THE WHIZ OF OZ

Who has a big nose and lives in the Emerald City?

The Wizard of Snozz.

✳ ✳ ✳

Dorothy: Never tease Munchkins.
Cowardly Lion: Why not?
Dorothy: Because they're short tempered.

✳ ✳ ✳

Why is it uncomfortable for the Tin Man to sit down?

Because he has to sit on a tin can.

**Why does the Cowardly
Lion live alone?**

He's such a chicken
he has no pride.

**Why does the Scarecrow
look like a hobo?**

His clothes are seedy.

**What did Dorothy wear when she
went scuba diving in Oz?**

Ruby flippers.

Which U.S. state is the Tin Man from?

Cansas.

Who lives in Oz and cooks chicken for Colonel Sanders?

The Frying Monkeys.

✳ ✳ ✳

What is a Munchkins favorite dessert?

Strawberry very short cake.

✳ ✳ ✳

What happened to the Munchkin who turned to a life of crime?

He became a small time crook.

✳ ✳ ✳

What is the quickest way out of Munchkin Land?

Take the short cut.

What did the hungry T-Rex say when he saw Munchkins at noontime?

Ah. Lunchkins are served.

❋ ❋ ❋

What job did the Munchkin get at the diner?

Short order cook.

❋ ❋ ❋

What do female Munchkins wear?
Mini skirts.

❋ ❋ ❋

What do you call a Munchkin after it gets stepped on by Godzilla?

A Crunch-kin!

What kind of briefs do male Munchkins wear?

Boxer short shorts.

* * *

What happened when the Scarecrow had a fight with the Tin Man?

The Scarecrow kicked his can.

NOTICE
The Tin Man likes heavy metal music.

Who lives in Oz, has magic powers, and is sticky?
Glenda the Glue Witch.

✳ ✳ ✳

Why didn't the Tin Man make it to the Emerald City?
He had to stop and rust.

✳ ✳ ✳

Why was the Tin Man upset?
The Scarecrow told him his can was too big.

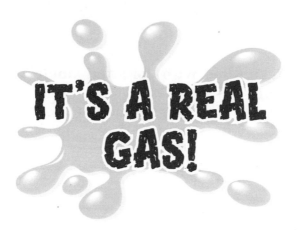

IT'S A REAL GAS!

What made the Garden of Eden smell bad?

The Adam bomb.

✻ ✻ ✻

Jack: This letter smells funny.
Zack: Maybe it came from a mail odor company.

What's filled with gold and smells awful?

Fart Knox.

✳ ✳ ✳

KNOCK! KNOCK!

Who's there?

Dots.

Dots who?

Dots a pile of cow manure.

✳ ✳ ✳

Miguel: Did Juan make the soccer team?

José: No. The stinking coach cut Juan.

KNOCK! KNOCK!

Who's there?
Paula.
Paula who?
Paula my finger, Luigi.

Jerry: Have you ever seen a karate expert break a board in half?

Barry: No. But I've heard a martial arts expert cut one.

was the motto of Teddy
Roosevelt Skunk?

Speak softly and carry a big stink.

* * *

How do you make a rump roast?

Put your cold behind too close to the
campfire.

* * *

**What do you need to work at a
sewage treatment plant?**

A turd grade education.

* * *

**What does the Norse hero Thor wear
beneath his armor?**

Thunderwear.

Hippy: Yo! Do you want to hear a funny noise, man?

Dippy: Is it totally hilarious, dude?

Hippy: Take it from me, it's a real gas.

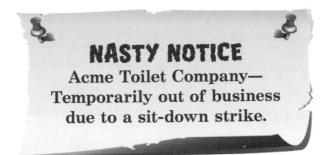

NASTY NOTICE
Acme Toilet Company—
Temporarily out of business
due to a sit-down strike.

What do you call an antelope with stomach gas?

A gnu farter.

What do you call a sheep with stomach gas?

Ewe stinker.

✳ ✳ ✳

KNOCK! KNOCK!

Who's there?

Toilet.

Toilet who?

Toilet a room you need to advertise that it's vacant.

SICK BUSINESS CARD

B.M. Flusher—

Bathroom plumbing expert

What do you get if you cross an angel with a skunk?

Heaven scent.

❋ ❋ ❋

KNOCK! KNOCK!

Who's there?

Ty Tea.

Ty Tea who?

Ty Tea Whitey Underwear!

❋ ❋ ❋

Man with Diarrhea: Where can a person go to the bathroom in this building?

Desk Clerk: Try the turd floor.

KNOCK! KNOCK!

Who's there?

Acid.

Acid who?

Acid it's rude to pass gas in public.

✳ ✳ ✳

Who was George Washington Smelly?

He was the Farter of our Country.

✳ ✳ ✳

What do you call a mob of people who just had chili for dinner?

A toxic crowd.

230

What Star Trek movie is about an angry clogged digestive system?
The Wrath of Khanstipation.

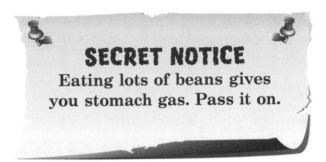

SECRET NOTICE
Eating lots of beans gives
you stomach gas. Pass it on.

KNOCK! KNOCK!
Who's there?
We leave.
We leave who?
We leave yourself at the next rest stop.

231

Son: Dad, I wouldn't let Fido lick your face like that.

Father: Why not? Fido is the family pet and he loves me.

Son: He also loves drinking water from the toilet bowl and he just quenched his thirst.

❋ ❋ ❋

Don: You smell like a skunk who has B.O.

Lon: That's a stinkin' lie.

❋ ❋ ❋

Gus: Should I cut the Swiss cheese?

Russ: No, hole it.

SIGN ON A SEWAGE TREATMENT PLANT

We love being in this stinkin' business.

Zeke: A skunk lives in that burrow.
Clem: Wow! I bet it's a real stink hole.

✳ ✳ ✳

KNOCK! KNOCK!

Who's there?

Bea Shore.

Bea Shore who?

Bea Shore to flush the toilet after you use it.

233

KNOCK! KNOCK!

Who's there?
The odor.
The odor who?
The odor you get, the wiser you become.

✳ ✳ ✳

What's the first thing to teach a young prince during potty training?
The importance of a royal flush.

✳ ✳ ✳

Then there was the ram who had a very sore neck. Every time he bumped into another ram, the meeting gave him a pain in the butt.

Two city kids were visiting their uncle's farm. One day they saw him driving a pickup truck full of manure.

"Where are you going with that?" one kid asked his uncle.

"I'm going to spread it on my corn," he explained.

"Yuk!" gasped the other kid. "At home we spread butter on our corn."

Who smells the worst at a wedding?
The farter of the bride.

✱ ✱ ✱

Mark: Why does this window glass smell so bad?
Clark: Maybe they're gas panes.

✱ ✱ ✱

Which sailor is the butt of a lot of jokes?
The Rear Admiral.

✱ ✱ ✱

What do you get when rabbits have stomach gas?
Hare pollution.

Which famous Egyptian ate a lot of beans?

King Toot.

* * *

Then there was the bathroom company that wanted to replace all toilets with urinals, but the public wouldn't stand for it.

* * *

KNOCK! KNOCK!

Who's there?

Adair.

Adair who?

Adair you to make a rude noise in class.

BEANS ON THE BRAIN
Beans, beans, the magical fruit;
the more you eat,
the more you toot!

What happens when you put beans in a car's gas tank?

Its horn toots.

✳ ✳ ✳

What do you get if you cross beans with apples?

Tootie Fruitie.

What day is it when a frog has stomach gas?

Hoppy Farter's Day.

✳ ✳ ✳

What do you get if you cross beans with a chewy candy?

Toot toot tootsie rolls.

✳ ✳ ✳

What do you get if you cross trumpets with beans?

Horns that go toot.

✳ ✳ ✳

How does Mr. Skunk call home?

He uses his smell phone.

When doesn't a skunk smell?
When it has a bad head cold.

✳ ✳ ✳

Mary: My porcelain doll is named Wynn.
Terry: Can I pick it up?
Mary: Yes, but be careful. Don't break Wynn.

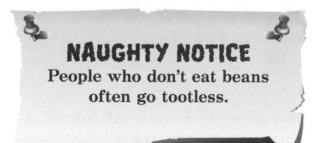

NAUGHTY NOTICE
People who don't eat beans often go tootless.

Lana: I just heard a
loud noise come
from your garden.
Donna: Relax. It was
just a sonic bloom.

**Which smelly general
almost conquered the world?**
Napoleon Bonafart.

How can you tell if a skunk has stomach gas?
    You can't.

✳ ✳ ✳

Dr. Smith: There is gas vapor in our new light bulbs.
Dr. Jones: Humph! Now I know watt stinks.

✳ ✳ ✳

Boss: Get busy and roll that wooden keg toward that truck.
Foreman: Let's go, men. It's time for a barrel movement.

GROSS US OUT!

What did Pinocchio say to the woodpecker?

Quit pecking my nose.

✳ ✳ ✳

What happened when Paul Bunyon told the Green Giant a really funny joke?

He laughed so hard he peed his plants.

What was the name of Elvis Hog's girlfriend?

Piggy Soo-ey.

What kind of bathrooms do pigs use in an emergency?

Pork-a-potties.

KNOCK! KNOCK!
Who's there?
Olive.
Olive who?
Olive to eat greasy foods.

✳ ✳ ✳

What did the angry orange say to the fruit fly?
Go suck a lemon!

✳ ✳ ✳

KNOCK! KNOCK!
Who's there?
Juno.
Juno who?
Juno your fly is down?

What do you hold in front of a carsick dog?

An arf barf bag.

✳ ✳ ✳

What do you call a pay bathroom?

A toll-let.

✳ ✳ ✳

Teacher: Johnny! That's disgusting! Take your finger out of your nose. How would you like it if I did that with my finger?

Johnny: Use your own nose, teacher.

✳ ✳ ✳

What's red with brown spots?

A tomato with freckles.

ANIMAL TRAINER
My dogs like sic humor.

Art: My dad owns a kennel and I have to clean up after the dogs.

Bart: That's not so bad. My dad owns a circus and I have to clean up after the elephants.

✳ ✳ ✳

What do you call the front of a clock covered with mozzarella cheese and pepperoni?

A pizza face.

247

What does a meteorologist announce after a thousand people eat chili with beans?

A wind warning.

* * *

Grandpa: Why are you eating your supper standing up?

Grandson: Mom told me never to sit down at the dinner table with dirty hands.

* * *

What do you do for a constipated computer?

Feed it lots of fiber optics.

Mother Robin: Eating worms is good for you.

Baby Robin: You don't expect me to swallow that, do you?

What did the booger say to Detective Nose and Officer Finger?

I dare you to pick me out of a lineup.

What does a rabbit use when it has an upset stomach?

A hare sickness bag.

Why do cats use deodorant?

To prevent purr-spiration odor.

FARM FRESH

Then there was the dirty, filthy vegetable farmer whose lettuce and cabbages had head lice.

Then there was the dirty, filthy corn farmer who never washed behind his ears.

Then there was the dirty, filthy tree farmer whose dogwoods had fleas.

Then there was the filthy rabbit farmer who never washed his dirty hares.

Then there was the dirty, filthy hog farmer whose house looked like a pig sty.

Then there was the uncouth farmer whose watermelons looked seedy.

Waiter: Did you like our boiled pig intestines platter?

Customer: No! Frankly I hate your guts.

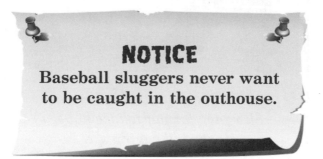

NOTICE
Baseball sluggers never want to be caught in the outhouse.

What's black and white and turns white and red?

An army zebra who is embarrassed about losing his stripes.

What does a polar bear eat that is black, white, red, yellow, and green?

A penguin with ketchup, mustard, and relish on it.

* * *

What do you call a nervous grizzly who writes plays?

Shakes Bear.

* * *

KNOCK! KNOCK!

Who's there?

Wool Under.

Wool Under who?

Wool Underwear itches!

What did the floor wax say to the floor?
Do you want to hear a good polish joke?

✳ ✳ ✳

Why is alphabet soup good for constipation?
It makes going E-Z.

✳ ✳ ✳

What do you call a half-dozen attack dogs?
A sic-pack.

✳ ✳ ✳

What do you ask a camel before serving it tea?
One lump or two?

How did the pig get a traffic ticket?
It ran through a slop sign.

✳ ✳ ✳

What's gray, has big ears, and weighs 500 pounds?
A mouse with a severe eating disorder.

✳ ✳ ✳

What did geeky ground say to his friend the cool shade?
Don't try to ditch me, pal.

✳ ✳ ✳

What did the booger say to the cat's box?
I'm the pick of the litter.

WHY DID YOU THROW UP?

I'm sick of your face, Mr. Clock.

I'm sick of your excuses, Mr. Tardy.

I'm sick of your tall stories, Mr. Writer.

I'm sick of having nothing, Mr. Zero.

*I'm sick of having so many bills,
Mr. Williams.*

*I'm sick of the same old routine,
Mr. Comedian.*

KNOCK! KNOCK!

Who's there?

Hugo.

Hugo who?

Hugo behind the bushes. I'll keep watch.

❋ ❋ ❋

What did the big pile of garbage say to the sanitation worker?

Thanks a heap, pal.

❋ ❋ ❋

Man: Hey, pal! You're all mixed up. You have socks on your hands.

Dumb Guy: Oh my gosh! Then I must have gloves on my feet!

What do you get if you cross bad jokes with boxer shorts?

Punderwear.

❋ ❋ ❋

What cheese did Dr. Frankenstein invent?

The Ugly Munster.

❋ ❋ ❋

What did the rusty pipe say to the plumber?

Excuse me. I have to take a leak.

❋ ❋ ❋

What do you call a flea-infested rabbit?

Bugs, Bugs, Bugs Bunny!

What did the angry watch say to the bully?

Stop making fun of my face.

＊ ＊ ＊

Senator: Did you hear the latest news broadcast? They reported that the President has a weak bladder.

Congressman: Let's find out who leaked that story to the press.

＊ ＊ ＊

KNOCK! KNOCK!

Who's there?

Coincide.

Coincide who?

Coincide and see if anyone is using the bathroom.

Doctor: You have claustrophobia. It's a fear of being shut up or closed in.

Jack: Gosh! I guess I'll have to start thinking outside the box.

✳ ✳ ✳

What did the Danish say to the coffee cake?

Get out of the bakery and take your crumby friends with you.

✳ ✳ ✳

What did the mosquito say to its psychologist?

You've got to help me. My life sucks.

KNOCK! KNOCK!

Who's there?

Hy Kant.

Hy Kant who?

Hy Kant hold it any longer. Open the bathroom door!

❋ ❋ ❋

What do you get if you cross a parrot with a pigeon?

A bird that apologizes for the mess it makes.

❋ ❋ ❋

Where do sheep post messages on the Internet?

Ewe Tube.

What do you eat with a hamburger in the streets of Paris?

French flies.

* * *

How did Mr. and Mrs. Octopus stroll down the lane?

Arm in arm, in arm, in arm, in arm.

* * *

What do you get if you cross a sewer line with a clock?

Sep-ticks.

Farmer Green: My cow won't give milk unless I tell her funny jokes.

Farmer Brown: That's udder nonsense.

KNOCK! KNOCK!

Who's there?

Atlas.

Atlas who?

Atlas I get to use the bathroom.

✳ ✳ ✳

What's big and hops around on one foot?

A kangaroo with a broken leg.

✳ ✳ ✳

Why did Mr. Clam lift weights?

He wanted to be a mussel man.

✳ ✳ ✳

Shepherd: I know a gangsta sheep who has a baa attitude.

How can you tell a happy motorcyclist?

By the bugs in his teeth.

✻ ✻ ✻

How do commuter teeth cross the Hudson River?

They take the tooth ferry.

✻ ✻ ✻

How can you tell if a stalk of corn has dandruff?

If you see corn flakes, it's dandruff.

✻ ✻ ✻

What sticky snack did Mother Cat make for her kittens?

Mice Crispie Treats.

Customer: Yuk! This hamburger tastes like dirt.
Waiter: What do you expect, sir, the meat was ground this morning.

Why didn't the magic lamp grant Aladdin his wish?
The dude just rubbed him the wrong way.

KNOCK! KNOCK!

Who's there?

Bret.

Bret who?

Bret as bad as yours needs strong
mouthwash.

✳ ✳ ✳

**Why wouldn't Mother Cyclops let her
son own a B.B. gun?**

She was afraid he'd shoot his eye
out.

✳ ✳ ✳

**What did the Cyclops say when he
felt tired?**

I think I'll get some shut eye.

Why did the Cyclops quit his teaching job?

He only had one pupil.

✳ ✳ ✳

What did the Cyclops say to his true love?

I only have eye for you.

✳ ✳ ✳

How does Sailor Cyclops reply to orders from his captain?

Aye, sir.

✳ ✳ ✳

What do you call a secret agent Cyclops?

Eye Spy.

King: Stay alert. A
     Cyclops is reported
     to be in the area.
Guard: What's a
     Cyclops?
King: A Cyclops is a giant,
     one-eyed monster.
Guard: I'll keep an eye out for it.

✳ ✳ ✳

**What did the ears of corn say to the
farmer?**

Stop stalking us.

✳ ✳ ✳

**What do you get if you cross a lemon
with a female deer?**

Some sour doe.

TONGUE TWISTED

Sheered sheep shouldn't sleep in sloppy stalls, Sherry Shepherd sighed.

Harry: Why are you sifting through a dumpster?

Larry: I want to get the pick of the litter.

✳ ✳ ✳

Why was the wristwatch so depressed?

Someone said it had an ugly face.

What did Mr. Centipede spend his life savings on?

Odor eaters for his shoes.

* * *

What do you call a European bathroom for swine?

A pigloo.

* * *

Doctor: You have an ego problem. What do you think of that?

Patient: Can I help it if I'm so great?

* * *

What do you get if you cross hippos with pigeons?

Some really messy car windshields.

Teacher: Wash your face. I can see what you had for breakfast this morning.

Student: Oh yeah. What did I have?

Teacher: Fried eggs.

Student: Wrong! I had that yesterday.

What do you get if you cross a dermatologist with a math teacher?
Complexion problems.

* * *

Teacher: Your handwriting is very sloppy.
Student: Don't blame me. I must have used a pig pen.

* * *

Why did Mrs. Goat make her baby climb on the outhouse roof?
She was potty training her kid.

* * *

What do angry bees use to exercise?
Swarm-up suits.

273

KNOCK! KNOCK!

Who's there?

Hairy Gnome.

Hairy Gnome who?

Hairy Gnome from your business trip.

Why did the forest rangers arrest Smokey for indecent exposure?

They caught him walking around in the woods bear naked.

Where do infected pimples wait for mass transportation to the doctor's office?

At the pus stop.

What do gorilla scouts sell?
Chocolate chimp cookies.

❋ ❋ ❋

What should you give an aardvark who has stomach gas?
Ant-acid.

❋ ❋ ❋

What parasitic bugs live on the moon?
Luna ticks.

❋ ❋ ❋

What's small, red and white, and hops?
A baby white rabbit with diaper rash.

What fairy story is about a nice tooshie and an ugly creature?
Booty and the Beast.

✳ ✳ ✳

What does a lion eat that's black and white and red all over?
A zebra with ketchup on it.

✳ ✳ ✳

What is the wackiest bug in the world?
The kook-roach.

✳ ✳ ✳

Where do skunks post messages on the Internet?
Phew Tube.

KNOCK! KNOCK!

Who's there?

Gas.

Gas who?

Gas who's coming to dinner.

✻ ✻ ✻

Lester: What do you get if you cross a football player with a centipede?

Chester: I don't know, but I bet it's good at kicking field goals.

✻ ✻ ✻

What did Convict Pimple say to Detective Fingers?

Don't try to squeeze a confession out of me.

KNOCK! KNOCK!

Who's there?

Howdy.

Howdy who?

Howdy get his zipper stuck?

✳ ✳ ✳

What did the grizzly bear swallow to soothe his stomachache?

Elk-a-seltzer.

Mike: Just because I talk to myself
doesn't mean I'm crazy.
Spike: Then why do you do it?
Mike: I'm the only person who will
listen to me.

❋ ❋ ❋

**What do you get when a firefly drops
its pants?**
Moon light.

❋ ❋ ❋

KNOCK! KNOCK!
Who's there?
Irma.
Irma who?
Irma teeth yellow from not brushing
enough?

279

KNOCK! KNOCK!

Who's there?

Alaska.

Alaska who?

Alaska if she has to use the bathroom before we leave.

GROSS BOOK TITLE

"How to Potty Train in Ten Easy Lessons—A to Do-Do List"

Why did the flies go to Hollywood?

To make some screen tests.

KNOCK! KNOCK!

Who's there?

Jamaica.

Jamaica who?

Jamaica funny noise in the boys' room?

✳ ✳ ✳

Charley: I attended grade school on a cruise ship.

Harley: Did you ever go to the head of the class?

✳ ✳ ✳

Sal: Excuse me. I heard you talking about toilet bowls. Do you mind if I interrupt?

Hal: No. As far as toilet bowls are concerned, you can jump in any time.

Boy: Dad, you should have named me Moron instead of Myron.

Father: Why would I do a silly thing like that, son?

Boy: Because that's what all of the kids in the neighborhood call me.

✳ ✳ ✳

Teacher: Please don't eat with your mouth open.

Student: If I don't open my mouth, how am I going to get the food in?

GROSS CONFESSIONS

*I know a math teacher
with gas problems.*

*I know a marathon racer
who has trouble with the runs.*

*I know a poultry farmer
who has really fowl breath.*

*I know a guy with a clogged nose
who smells bad.*

Student: Yesterday, Farmer Gray got some good news and jumped in excretion.

Teacher: Don't you mean he jumped in excitement?

Student: No. He jumped into the air and came down in a pile of cow manure.

✳ ✳ ✳

Paul: My friend and I were stocking shelves at the grocery when the local bully came in to buy soup.

Saul: What happened?

Paul: He knocked us on our cans.

What's green, bumpy, and boring?
A pickle making a campaign speech.

GROSS DEFINITION
Go-Go Girl–
a female dancer
with a weak bladder.

What's green, bumpy, and smells?
A pickle with stomach gas.

Editor: The last word in your book is "but."

Writer: It's a rear ending.

✳ ✳ ✳

Dumb Athlete: How much will you pay me to play for your team?

Coach: Nothing.

Dumb Athlete: Double your offer and you've got a deal.

✳ ✳ ✳

Wife: Would you eat frogs' legs if I served them to you for dinner?

Husband: Yes. I'd jump at the chance.

HOW'S BUSINESS?

Fruit Peddler—
"It's rotten."

Bait Salesman—
"It bites."

Scrub Brush Salesman—
"It's in the toilet."

Barf Bag Producer—
"It's putrid."

Scented Candle Maker—
"It reeks."

GROSS NOTICE
Mrs. Kangaroo's lazy baby boy was a pouch potato.

Mary: Gus is having fun at this amusement park.
Barry: Is that true? Are you having fun gus?

✳ ✳ ✳

Derrick: Why is Jacque scratching?
Eric: Maybe he has Jacque itch.

KNOCK! KNOCK!

Who's there?

Cayuse.

Cayuse who?

Cayuse the bathroom? It's an emergency.

Foreman to Employee: Carry this case of cow intestines over to the sausage factory and be careful not to spill your guts.

❋ ❋ ❋

Rob: I just sent a skunk up in a hot air balloon.

Bob: Wow! You really know how to raise a stink.

❋ ❋ ❋

What do you call baby chicks lined up one behind the other in a bathroom?

A row of toilet peepers.

How do cats like to watch their favorite movies?

In litter box format.

✳ ✳ ✳

Which parasite gets good grades in math?

The arithme-tick.

✳ ✳ ✳

What do you get if you cross boogers with a wristwatch?

A goo goo clock.

✳ ✳ ✳

What do you get if you lock Bambi in an icebox?

A frigideer.

TONGUE TWISTED
Farmer Phil Farve flushed
four flat fish fast.

Why did the clock go to the psychologist?

It had a nervous tick.

✳ ✳ ✳

Which skeleton was a frontier scout?

Daniel Bone.

What do you call a penniless person in a bathroom?

Toilet pauper.

* * *

What weighs 1,000 pounds and wears a diaper?

A baby hippo.

* * *

Scissors: Do you need some tape?
Wrapping Paper: Yes. Stick it to me.

* * *

What's black and white and red?

A strawberry penguin sundae with a cherry on top.

Why did the numeral rush into the bathroom?

It had to go number two.

＊ ＊ ＊

What's worse than an elephant with dirt behind its ears?

A giraffe with a filthy neck.

＊ ＊ ＊

How do you stop a skunk from smelling bad?

Use an ex-stink-guisher.

＊ ＊ ＊

What kind of bathroom does a cowboy use?

He uses the westroom.

How can a cowboy tell when he needs a stronger underarm deodorant?

During a holdup, an outlaw will order him to keep his arms down.

Egyptian #1: Queen Cleopatra's pet dog slobbers all over everything.

Egyptian #2: I know that hound is the drool of the Nile.

✳ ✳ ✳

Grandfather: Your house is spic and span. The floors are clean enough to eat off of.

Granddaughter: I'm glad you feel that way, Grandpa. Your sandwich fell off of your plate in the kitchen.

✳ ✳ ✳

Godzilla: What did you have for dinner?

Moby Dick: Fish and ships.

Waiter: This is our pig farmer lunch
   special.
Customer: Do people actually eat this
   slop?

✳ ✳ ✳

**What do you get if you cross a
centipede with an ostrich?**
   I don't know, but if a hungry lion
catches it, he tears it limb from limb
from limb from limb. . .

✳ ✳ ✳

Tillie: Why do you have all of that gook
   on your face?
Millie: I just finished a makeup test.

KNOCK! KNOCK!

Who's there?

European.

European who?

European every ten minutes. Do you have weak kidneys?

* * *

Mother: Would you like to try this nice creamed spinach?

Son: No. But I'd like to see the cow it came from.

* * *

What did the gulf say to the sick river?

Please cover your mouth when you sneeze.

GROSS SIGN
Acme Laxative Company—
We don't work irregular
business hours.

Kelly: If you go into that small grocery
 store, you'll start to itch.
Nellie: Why?
Kelly: It's a flea market.

❋ ❋ ❋

**What did the angry witch say to the
sheep?**
 A pox on ewe.

299

What's red and white and wooly?
A sheep with a pox on it.

✳ ✳ ✳

Tarzan: Look at all of the ivory on that bull elephant?
Jane: Now there's a good example of multi-tusking.

✳ ✳ ✳

Student: I was playing a miniature harmonica in music class and I swallowed it.
School Nurse: Thank goodness you don't play the tuba.

Student: This milk tastes sour.
Cafeteria Lady: Drink it. It'll make
you feel bitter.

✳ ✳ ✳

Lady: I don't like the look of the mold
in this house.
Real Estate Agent: Relax. If you live
here long enough, it'll grow on you.

✳ ✳ ✳

Waiter: This platter is our pole vault
special.
Customer: I wouldn't touch that food
with a ten foot pole.

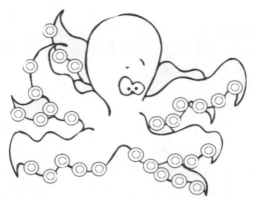

What did the octopus say to the centipede?

Hey, pal! Your feet stink!

✳ ✳ ✳

What did the centipede answer?

Oh yeah? Well you need more underarm deodorant.

Ken: I went to sanitation management
  class last week.
Len: What happened?
Ken: I got thrown out.

✳ ✳ ✳

**Which play do pimply baseball
players hate the most?**
  The squeeze play.

✳ ✳ ✳

What do cows with acne give?
  Pimple cream.

✳ ✳ ✳

**What do you get if you cross bunnies
with onions and potatoes?**
  Bunions on your toes.

Uncle: Ick! I'll make you a deal. If you don't blow your nose in your right hand anymore, I'll buy you an ice cream cone.

Nephew: It's a deal, Unc. Let's shake on it.

* * *

Waiter: This platter is our dumpster special.

Customer: Who eats this junk?

* * *

What did Fonzie Rabbit say to his bunny girlfriend?

Don't tease your hare.

Why did Mr. Red Squirrel sue Mr. Gray Squirrel?

It was just your typical nut case.

✳ ✳ ✳

KNOCK! KNOCK!

Who's there?

Wart.

Wart who?

Wart do you want me to do? Beg?

✳ ✳ ✳

What did one cat say to the other after using the litter box?

This is dirty business and we have to cover it up.

Coach #1: My distance runner needs a tissue.
Coach #2: Why?
Coach #1: She has a runny nose.

❉ ❉ ❉

Mr. Smith: They just raised the price of stomach antacid.
Mr. Jones: The price of gas is going up everywhere.

STOMACH CHURNING CHUCKLES

What has gills, a clipboard, wears sneakers, and is found in a school gym?

A fish ed teacher.

✳ ✳ ✳

Nick: Do you mind if I stick my finger up my nose?

Rick: No. Go ahead and pick, Nick.

Who puts out forest fires and isn't easy to see?

Smokey the Blur.

* * *

Alfie: I know a tavern owner who raises rabbits on the side.

Ralphie: I guess he has a lot of Inn grown hares.

How do you autograph a leopard?
Sign on the dotted lion.

* * *

How do you make a dirty watch crystal mad?
Spit on its face.

* * *

Lady: I like lots of lawn ornaments.
Neighbor: I know. Sometimes when I look at your yard, it makes me Gnomesick.

* * *

What did the British redcoat say to the American minuteman?
You have a revolting face.

FACE THE HORRIBLE TRUTH

Comedian . . .
*Your face is so funny
it makes me want to laugh.*

Doctor . . .
Your face just makes me plain sick.

Fruit Grower . . .
Your face is plum ugly.

Optometrist . . .
Your face is an awful sight.

Comic . . .
Your face makes me gag.

Police Officer . . .
*It should be a crime
to have a face like that.*

Movie Director . . .
*When I see your face
I do a double take.*

What do you get if you put a clock on a tree?

Wood ticks.

❋ ❋ ❋

KNOCK! KNOCK!

Who's there?

Icon.

Icon who?

Icon not keep any food down.

TONGUE TWISTED

Smelly Sally sells soft satin sheep sheets.

KNOCK! KNOCK!

Who's there?

Belle Chen.

Belle Chen who?

Belle Chen is a way to release stomach gas.

* * *

What do hero skunks perform?

Smelly feats.

* * *

How do you make a dirty watch crystal mad?

Spit on its face.

Camper #1: Why are you running so fast?

Camper #2: Don't look now, but there's a bear behind.

✳ ✳ ✳

KNOCK! KNOCK!
Who's there?

Len.

Len who?

Len me some change for the pay toilet.

✳ ✳ ✳

Why wouldn't the ram kiss the ewe on her birthday?

She had baa breath.

Mack: How did your dog break his front
    legs?
Zack: He did it trying to bury a bone.
Mack: Where?
Zack: In the middle of the parking lot.

Father: Why did you put ants in your
   sister's bed?
Son: Because I'm afraid to pick up
   roaches.

✳ ✳ ✳

Why did the air rifle get rusty?
   It was filled with cry B.B.'s.

✳ ✳ ✳

Why did the lawn get grass plugs?
   It had a reseeding hair problem.

✳ ✳ ✳

**How can you tell if a river is only a
baby?**
   If it's a baby, it'll have a soggy
bottom.

What do you call the owner of a flower shop who can't move?

A petrified florist.

＊ ＊ ＊

Why was the hobo wearing a bathing suit?

He was going dumpster diving.

＊ ＊ ＊

KNOCK! KNOCK!

Who's there?

Gross.

Gross who?

Gross-ery bills are getting higher and higher.

GROSS NOTICE
Free pet monster to good
home...will eat anything...
especially likes children.

Why did the freeway have a mild heart attack?

It had clogged arteries.

* * *

What did the infected pimple say to the wart?

My head aches so bad I think it's going to burst.

What do adult witches drink while watching baseball games?

Cold brewskics.

✳ ✳ ✳

Which space hero is always sick to his stomach?

Puke Skywalker.

✳ ✳ ✳

What did the body say to the vomit?

I just can't stomach you.

✳ ✳ ✳

Which cuddly yellow bear smells bad?

Winnie the Poo Poo.

Who throws up a lot and kills blood-sucking monsters?

Barfy the Vampire Slayer.

KNOCK! KNOCK!

Who's there?

Hyphen.

Hyphen who?

Hyphen waiting to use the bathroom for a long time.

✳ ✳ ✳

Why did the stupid poultry farmer go broke?

All of the roosters he bought refused to lay eggs.

✳ ✳ ✳

Dex: I save newspaper stories about human toes.

Lex: Do you have any toenail clippings?

TONGUE TWISTED

Silly Sally Smits sold seven short salesmen smelly steak sauce.

Captain Ron: Gosh! The mouth of that river is really swollen.

Captain Don: Haven't you ever seen a river bloat before?

✳ ✳ ✳

Why did the stupid kid fall out of his tree house?

He forgot there was no basement.

Why couldn't the stupid chef boil water?

He didn't remember the recipe.

What union group did Butch Cassidy and Billy the Kid belong to?

The World Rustling Federation.

SICK SANTA LAUGHS

What do you get if you cross a skunk with Santa Claus?
Scent Nick.

What does Santa do when it's time to take out the garbage?
He gives it the ol' heave ho ho.

Who always crashes into buildings while pulling Santa's sleigh?
Rudork the Red-Nosed Reindeer.

Who goes "Ho! Whoa! Ouch!"?
Santa falling off a rooftop.

＊ ＊ ＊

Why did stupid Santa take his reindeer to the dentist?
Because they all had buck teeth.

＊ ＊ ＊

What wears a red suit and lives in the ocean?
Santa Crab Claws.

＊ ＊ ＊

What wears a red suit and weighs two tons?
Santa Elephant.

Whose house is always sloppy during the December holidays?

Mary Chris Mess.

＊ ＊ ＊

Who has pointed ears, wears a green jumpsuit, and sings rock and roll?

Elfis Presley.

＊ ＊ ＊

What does Santa use to unclog his toilet?

Drain Ho-Ho-Ho!

＊ ＊ ＊

Why does Paul Bunyon like the month of December?

He loves to go Christmas chopping.

What's furry and has big fangs and a nose that lights up?

Rudolf the Red-Nosed Werewolf.

What did Mr. Stupid find in his stockings on Christmas morning?

His smelly feet. He sleeps with his socks on.

Why doesn't a miser mind getting coal in his Christmas stocking?

It helps reduce his winter heating bills.

* * *

What do you call Alaskan skunks?

North polecats.

What does an obese snowman have around his waist?

A spare snow tire.

Why did the snowman use a dandruff shampoo?

He had flakes on his shoulders.

What has pointed ears, is six feet tall, and has lots of muscles?
An elf on steroids.

✳ ✳ ✳

What do you call elf gangsters?
A gang of small-time crooks.

✳ ✳ ✳

Why don't elves exercise more?
It leaves them short of breath.

✳ ✳ ✳

What do you get if you cross the Green Giant with Santa Claus?
Someone who gets pea hoed over things.

Mother: Jimmy! What's a dead fish doing in your coat pocket?

Jimmy: Oops! Yesterday I took our pet goldfish out for a walk and forgot to put him back in the bowl.

✳ ✳ ✳

What's the best way to catch Moby Dick?

Bait a ship's anchor with a three hundred pound worm.

✳ ✳ ✳

When does a little green man from Venus turn red?

When you tell him the zipper of his space pants is down.

What did the UFO fan say when he stepped in manure?

I just had a close encounter of the turd kind.

* * *

How can you embarrass an alien traveling through space?

Tell him Uranus is showing.

* * *

What do you get if you cross property ownership papers with a school of tuna?

Deed fish.

How did the dumb athletes break their feet?

They played soccer with a bowling ball.

* * *

How does a dumb student cheat on an oral exam?

He sits behind the smartest kid in class so he can look over his shoulder.

* * *

Man: Every time I see a strange dog, I throw up. What's wrong with me, Doctor?

Doctor: You have cur sickness.

KNOCK! KNOCK!

Who's there?

Owl.

Owl who?

Owl scrub the bathroom bowl tomorrow.

✳ ✳ ✳

Rocco: I'm the bravest man in the world. There isn't a cowardly bone in my body.

Marco: That's big talk for a man who has yellow teeth.

✳ ✳ ✳

What do you call a dumb lumberjack who can't find his tools?

A saw loser.

What does Santa shout when he goes fox hunting?

Tally Ho! Ho! Ho!

✳ ✳ ✳

What does Attila put in his car?

Hunleaded gas.

✳ ✳ ✳

KNOCK! KNOCK!

Who's there?

Amos.

Amos who?

Amos stop wiping my nose on my sleeve.

What are the two hottest bugs in the world?

A cricket match and a firefly.

✳ ✳ ✳

KNOCK! KNOCK!

Who's there?

Hubie.

Hubie who?

Hubie a good boy and eat your liver and onions.

Which woodsman is very athletic?
The lumberjock.

✳ ✳ ✳

Why did the squirrel pretend to be crazy?
He wanted to live in a nut house.

✳ ✳ ✳

What's black and white and yellow?
A penguin with jaundice.

✳ ✳ ✳

What parts of the Earth smell the worst?
Turd World Countries.

KNOCK! KNOCK!

Who's there?

Jess.

Jess who?

Jess throw out this loaf of bread. It's moldy.

✳ ✳ ✳

Why did the rabbits go to the emergency room?

Bad hare cuts.

✳ ✳ ✳

Why did the corn farmer hire a prizefighter?

He wanted someone to box his ears.

How do you arrest a park chair?
Get a bench warrant.

✳ ✳ ✳

KNOCK! KNOCK!
Who's there?
Pool.
Pool who?
Pool my finger one more time.

✳ ✳ ✳

Mr. Smith: I heard the bathrooms on the top floor of this building are twice as big as the one on the bottom floor.
Mr. Jones: That's just a silly wash rumor.

KNOCK! KNOCK!

Who's there?

Hannah.

Hannah who?

Hannah me some bathroom tissue. This roll is empty.

✳ ✳ ✳

Girl College Student: Why is your arm in a cast?

Boy College Student: Spring break.

✳ ✳ ✳

Terry: How's your job testing birthday candles?

Gerry: It blows.

Man: How did you catch that giant fish?
Boy: I used a skunk lure and the fish
took the bait hook, line, and stinker.

**Which lawn ornament is a private
detective?**
Sherlock Gnomes.

What did the sanitation worker say to the angry garbage man?

Stop talking trash to me!

✳ ✳ ✳

Farm Expert: Do you want to discuss soil?

Farmer: Yes. But don't use any dirty words in front of my children.

SICK BOOK CLUB

"How to Avoid Foot Odor"
by S. Mel Feet

"Proper Bathroom Use"
by Donna P. Hare.

Sally: Do cats get runny noses?
Vet: Sometimes they have a problem
with excess mewcus.

❋ ❋ ❋

Farmer Brown: I heard your vegetable
garden failed this year.
Farmer Gray: Yes, but don't give me
any of your crop because of it.

❋ ❋ ❋

Farmer: My cow has a runny nose.
Vet: Don't worry. It's just moocus.

❋ ❋ ❋

**What has antlers, breathes fire, and
is covered with chocolate?**
A deer devil's food cake.

What do you get if you cross elephants with termites?

I don't know, but it chews huge holes in the woodwork.

✳ ✳ ✳

Why did the Earth get mad during the lunar eclipse?

His closest friend mooned him.

✳ ✳ ✳

Chester: How polluted is the Atlantic Ocean?

Lester: It must be pretty polluted. I just saw a school of flying fish migrating toward the Pacific.

KNOCK! KNOCK!

Who's there?

Phil T.

Phil T. who?

Phil T. hands need to be washed.

✳ ✳ ✳

What buzzes when you chew it?

Bumble gum.

✳ ✳ ✳

What do you get if you cross digestion with a math teacher?

Stomach problems.

KNOCK! KNOCK!

Who's there?

Farthing.

Farthing who?

Farthing in public is considered vulgar.

✳ ✳ ✳

Mother: Doctor, my son swallowed a pocket watch. What should I do?

Doctor: Find him a quiet place to pass the time.

✳ ✳ ✳

Farley: I heard that you always fall asleep on the job.

Harley: That's just a rest rumor.

SICK QUESTION
Do postal workers have to clean the letter box?

KNOCK! KNOCK!
Who's there?
Dotty.
Dotty who?
Dotty restrooms should be cleaned up.

✳ ✳ ✳

Why did the rooster get detention?
He used fowl language in class.

Bob: Why is there a pile of dead bugs lying by the pond?
Rob: It's toad kill.

Student: I threw up when I saw the grades on my report card.
Teacher: What's wrong with him, nurse?
Nurse: It's a case of C-sickness.

What do you get if you cross an athlete with a weak bladder, and a T.V. network?
ESPPN.

How did Captain Hook go blind in one eye?

He used the wrong hand to put in his contact lens.

KNOCK! KNOCK!
Who's there?
Kenny.
Kenny who?
Kenny hurry up in there? I can't hold it!

What goes "Ho! Ho! Yeow!"?

Santa Claus sliding down a chimney with a fire in it.

THE END OF THE LAUGHING LINE

Mr. Sandwich—*He went out like a hero.*

Ms. Gossip—*There's no more to tell.*

Mr. Payne—*He will be sorely missed.*

Mr. Retail—*He paid the ultimate price.*

Ms. Memory—*She won't be soon forgotten.*

Mr. Stupor—*His last daze were happy.*

Mr. Lemon—*His life had a bitter ending.*

Mr. Electric—*His passing came as a real shock.*

Ms. Hair Color—*She dyed bravely.*

Mr. Splinter—*He left behind a lot of friends.*

Ms. Math—*The sum total of her accomplishments is impressive.*

Mr. Money—*His last days were well spent.*

Mr. Quarterback—*Sports fans will mourn his passing.*

351

Who is the grossest monster in the world?

Slobzilla.

✳ ✳ ✳

Barry: I know a restaurant where we can eat dirt cheap.

Mary: Ick! Who wants to eat dirt at any price?

✳ ✳ ✳

Why did the pirates steal a bathtub?

It was their bathing booty.

✳ ✳ ✳

John: Name two loud stooges and a soft-spoken one.

Lon: Moe, Laryngitis, and Curly.

SICK REQUESTS

Mr. Skeleton—
Give me a break!

Mr. Hangman—
Cut me some slack!

Mr. Cliff—
Back off, will ya?

Mr. Clock—
Get out of my face!

Sal: What's on today's menu?
Hal: We're having roasted water fowl
and fried pastry for dessert.
Sal: Yippie! Duck and doughnuts.

✳ ✳ ✳

Why was Mr. Bubblegum so upset?
He got chewed out by his boss.

What do you call the rear part of a flying insect that produces honey?
A bee hind.

✳ ✳ ✳

Customer: Yuk! I can't eat this disgusting stew. Call the manager.
Waiter: It's no use, sir. He won't touch this slop either.

Lana: Do you like my ponytail?
Donna: Not really.
Lana: I think wearing my hair in a
ponytail makes me look smart.
Donna: Well, consider this. A ponytail
is usually connected to a horse's
behind.

✳ ✳ ✳

**What is a werewolf's favorite
televised sporting event?**

Full Moonday Night Football.

✳ ✳ ✳

**Why should you always flush your
toilet?**

Flushing does your bathroom a whirl
of good.

GROSS DEFINITION
Toilet flush—
down time.

What do you call an atomic cow?
  A mooclear device.

✳ ✳ ✳

Who made Cinderella Cow's dreams come true?
  Her Dairy Godmother.

SICK BOOK REVIEW
"Charlotte's Web"—
The story of pig's feat.

Judy: How in the world did you fail an IQ test?

Rudy: Easy. I didn't study for it.

✳ ✳ ✳

Show me a chef at a racetrack who loves to sample hotdogs . . . and I'll show you a guy who has a real knack for picking wieners.

Waiter: This breakfast platter is our joggers' special.
Customer: The eggs look too runny to eat.

* * *

What do you get if you cross a nuclear weapon with tight underwear?

An atomic wedgie.

* * *

Mrs. Bear: Junior got sent home from first grade today.
Mr. Bear: Why?
Mrs. Bear: He brought a skunk to school for show and smell.

Waiter: Try our spicy chili. It's our
football touchdown special.
Customer: No thanks. I don't want any
end zone trouble.

✳ ✳ ✳

**How does a plumber fix clogged
drainpipes?**
He hits them with a sludgehammer.

SICK NOTICE
Overweight androids have
big robutts.

Daughter: I only threw up a tiny bit.
Mother: That's weegurgitation.

Picnic Table: Why does the patio smell so bad?
Deck Chair: Blame it on the barbecue grill. It has gas.

TAKE YOUR PICK OF PLUMBERS...

Hughes A. Plunger
Hugo Frequently
Phil D. Tank
U. Ken Peenow

NOTICE

Basketball stars who don't use enough cologne have foul odor problems.

Why do gorillas have big nostrils?
Because they have big fingers.

✳ ✳ ✳

Bobby: How do you like my book of bathroom jokes?
Robby: It really stinks.
Bobby: Is that an insult or a compliment?

363

Ben: Flies must be poisonous to eat.
Len: Why do you say that?
Ben: Frogs eat them and they always
croak.

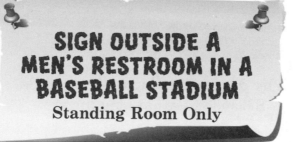

**SIGN OUTSIDE A
MEN'S RESTROOM IN A
BASEBALL STADIUM**
Standing Room Only

Belle: Do spoiled teen stars use public
restrooms?
Nell: No. They use private bratrooms.

What has fangs, is covered with fur and flies?

A dead werewolf.

✳ ✳ ✳

Why was the zombie sad at the New Year's Eve celebration?

He couldn't be the life of the party no matter how hard he tried.

✳ ✳ ✳

What did the fly paper say to the fly?

Hey, pal! Stick around for a while.

✳ ✳ ✳

Hal: Does a volcano use the bathroom?
Cal: No. It goes to the lava-tory.

GROSS NAMES

Hal B. Indaloo
Kenny Holdit
Missy Diapers
BeBe Wipes
A. Lotta Crop
Maye I. Gonow

What did the hungry werewolf say to Mr. Skeleton?

It's been nice gnawing you.

✳ ✳ ✳

What did the angry tree say to the busy beavers?

Why don't you guys get off my bark.

✳ ✳ ✳

KNOCK! KNOCK!

Who's there?

Asinine.

Asinine who?

Asinine comes after asieight when you're counting mules.

HOOKY HILARITY

Why didn't Captain Hook graduate from Neverland High School?

He spent too much time playing hooky.

✳ ✳ ✳

What did Captain Hook say to his first mate as he grabbed him?

Now do you get my point?

✳ ✳ ✳

How did Captain Hook cut his cheek?

He scratched his face with the wrong hand.

How did Captain Hook meet Mrs. Hook?

Friends hooked them up.

✳ ✳ ✳

How much did Captain Hook pay the saleslady for his new ship?

Sticker price.

✳ ✳ ✳

What did Hook say when he was offered the job of captain?

I'll take a stab at it.

✳ ✳ ✳

How does Captain Hook fish?

He baits his hook and sticks his arm in the water.

How does Captain Hook make enough money to pay his pirate crew?

By hook or by crook.

Where does Captain Hook hang his coat?

On a hook in the closet.

Jolly: Is Captain Hook a good golfer?
Roger: No. He hooks every shot.

What does Captain Hook use to cut a sirloin?

A meat hook and a steak knife.

How did Captain Hook puncture his good hand?

He went to a play and clapped too hard when it was over.

GROSS DEFINITION
Proctology—
a tushie job.

How does a witch keep her mode of transportation smelling nice?

She uses broom freshener.

What did the medical examiner say when they exhumed the wrong body?

We've made a grave mistake.

✳ ✳ ✳

What did Mrs. Corn Farmer say to Mr. Corn Farmer?

Stop picking your big ears.

✳ ✳ ✳

KNOCK! KNOCK!

Who's there?

Hole.

Hole who?

Hole your nose when you go into the bathroom or you'll be sorry.

Customer: Do you have tomato soup on your menu again today?
Waiter: No sir. We clean our menus every night.

✳ ✳ ✳

What did Mr. Corn Farmer reply to Mrs. Corn Farmer?

Speak up! I can't hear you. My ears are full of wax.

✳ ✳ ✳

What do you call Bruce Wayne's secret sink?

A batroom fixture.

NOTICE
There's nothing more gross than a carpenter who bites his nails.

KNOCK! KNOCK!
Who's there?
Orange.
Orange who?
Orange you gonna flush the toilet?

375

KNOCK! KNOCK!
Who's there?
I. Aida.
I. Aida who?
I. Aida bug and now I'm sick to my stomach.

❋ ❋ ❋

Sally: My pet rabbit fell in the mud.
Cally: Well, go home and wash your filthy hare.

❋ ❋ ❋

Tim: Ugh! I just swallowed a duck feather!
Jim: Would you like some water to wash it down?

Wendal: My dad said we can't use the bathroom in our mobile home while it's moving.

Kendal: Oh, so you always stop and go while on vacation.

✳ ✳ ✳

Sal: Can you name a sloppy composer?

Hal: Piggy Bach.

✳ ✳ ✳

KNOCK! KNOCK!

Who's there?

A. Smelter.

A. Smelter who?

A. Smelter perfume and it made me puke.

What did the toilet paper shout in the University of Alabama bathroom?

Roll crimson tide.

* * *

What rodent do you always find in the bathroom?

The lavatory rat.

* * *

KNOCK! KNOCK!

Who's there?

Peas.

Peas who?

Peas curb your dog and clean up after it.

KNOCK! KNOCK!

Who's there?

Sewer.

Sewer who?

Sewer if she refuses to pay her plumbing bill.

✳ ✳ ✳

KNOCK! KNOCK!

Who's there?

Hominy.

Hominy who?

Hominy times do I have to tell you to brush your teeth every morning.

379

SICK QUESTION
Do catfish use waterproof litter boxes?

Son: Uncle Joe just gave me a pet skunk.

Mother: That's nice, but you can't keep it in the house because of the awful smell.

Son: That's okay, Mom. The skunk won't care what our house smells like.

What is a parasite's favorite winter sport?

Lice hockey.

✳ ✳ ✳

Billy: My pet boa constrictor loves you. Can he give you a big hug?

Milly: No way! He might love me to death.

✳ ✳ ✳

KNOCK! KNOCK!

Who's there?

Tish.

Tish who?

Tish is an emergency! Hurry up in there.

This is what knights of old wore in battle. It's called a suit of armor. Any questions?

Little Boy: Yes. How do you unzip it to go to the bathroom?

❋ ❋ ❋

KNOCK! KNOCK!

Who's there?

Al.

Al who?

Al pee my pants if you don't open the bathroom door.

❋ ❋ ❋

What do you get if you cross toilet paper with a surfer?

Wipe out.

RF

Which army unit is the butt o
of military jokes?

The rear guard.

NOTICE
Acme Laxative
Incorporated—
we're the company to call
when the going gets tough.

KNOCK! KNOCK!

Who's there?

I. Betty.

I. Betty who?

I. Betty throws up after eating that slop.

383

What's red and falls down the chimney on Christmas Eve?

Santa Klutz.

✳ ✳ ✳

Why did the toilet paper roll down the hill?

Because it wanted to get to the bottom.

✳ ✳ ✳

Harry: What happened when a swarm of locusts fell into the river basin?

Larry: The river got sick. After all, no one likes to have bugs in their mouth.

KNOCK! KNOCK!

Who's there?

Arch.

Arch who?

Yuk! I told you not to sneeze all over me.

✳ ✳ ✳

What was the hungry beetle doing in the corn field?

Going in one ear and out the other.

✳ ✳ ✳

What's really tall, has fangs, and sucks blood out of hospitals?

The Vampire State Building.

Tony: Am I really that dumb?
Joanie: Let's put it this way. If brains were fertilizer, you couldn't raise a stink.

✳ ✳ ✳

What happened to the ship made of toilet paper?

It went to the bottom of the sea.

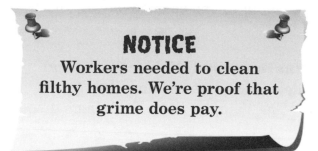

NOTICE
Workers needed to clean filthy homes. We're proof that grime does pay.

KNOCK! KNOCK!

Who's there?

Elsie.

Elsie who?

Elsie if the toilet is still running.

✳ ✳ ✳

Jill: My St. Bernard puppy has a pedigree.

Will: Oh! So you have papers for it?

Jill: Yup. They're all over the house.

✳ ✳ ✳

What do you call a big fight between minks, rabbits, and foxes?

A fur brawl.

KNOCK! KNOCK!

Who's there?

Halo.

Halo who?

Halo! Is anyone in that bathroom stall?

✳ ✳ ✳

What should you know before you invest in toilet paper?

What's the bottom line.

✳ ✳ ✳

What did one polluted river say to the other?

You have a mouth like a sewer.

KNOCK! KNOCK!

Who's there?

Wider.

Wider who?

Wider we always get stuck with scrubbing the bathroom bowl?

What did the toilet paper say to the bartender?

Bottoms up!

✳ ✳ ✳

Why did the toilet paper go to a casino?

It wanted to roll some dice.

What part of a movie does Mr. Toilet Paper like best?

The credit roll.

* * *

KNOCK! KNOCK!

Who's there?

Germ Ann.

Germ Ann who?

Germ Ann measles make you break out.

* * *

What do you get if a stag runs into a forest fire?

Hart burn.

Doctor: I think you have poison ivy.
Patient: Are you sure that's not a rash
diagnosis?

KNOCK! KNOCK!

Who's there?

Isadore.

Isadore who?

Isadore to the restroom unlocked?

* * *

What do you get if you cross a stag with math homework?

Hart problems.

* * *

KNOCK! KNOCK!

Who's there?

Izzy.

Izzy who?

Izzy gonna stay in the bathroom all day?

KNOCK! KNOCK!

Who's there?

Discus.

Discus who?

Discus-ting jokes are not funny.

✳ ✳ ✳

KNOCK! KNOCK!

Who's there?

Opie.

Opie who?

Opie remembers to flush the toilet.

BATHROOM RIDDLERS

Why was the toilet paper so mad?
Someone ripped it off.

✳ ✳ ✳

What does Bruce Wayne use to blow his nose?
Batroom tissue.

SICK DEFINITION
Toilet paper in a pay toilet—a roll of quarters.

What time is it when you have diarrhea?

Sick turdy.

❋ ❋ ❋

How can you rest easy when you have a wedgie?

Pick your seat carefully.

What did the fishing line say to the bass?

Bite me, stupid!

✳ ✳ ✳

KNOCK! KNOCK!

Who's there?

Fours.

Fours who?

Fours yourself to go to the bathroom before we leave.

✳ ✳ ✳

How long does it take an idiot to tie his shoes?

One minute to tie the laces and three hours to undo the knots.

Why did the idiot put bullets in the oven?

He thought it was a pistol range.

✳ ✳ ✳

What do you get if you cross a gypsy with a skunk?

A fortune smeller.

✳ ✳ ✳

KNOCK! KNOCK!

Who's there?

Fine.

Fine who?

Fine a place in the bushes to go to the bathroom.

New Wife: What's wrong, honey? Don't you like the breakfast I made? Did I use too much pepper?

New Husband: No, dear. My oatmeal is fine.

※ ※ ※

What do you get if you cross stomach gas with plastic wrap?

Bubble wrap.

※ ※ ※

What's the best thing to do if you step in cow poo?

Take a load off your feet.

399

KNOCK! KNOCK!

Who's there?

Wattle.

Wattle who?

Wattle I do if the gas station has no restroom?

* * *

What kind of underwear do reporters wear?

New briefs.

* * *

What do you get if you cross toilet paper with knives?

Roller blades.

KNOCK! KNOCK!

Who's there?

Eel.

Eel who?

Eel be sick to his stomach if he eats the greasy hamburger.

❉ ❉ ❉

What are purple and red and swim in the ocean?

A grape jelly fish and a strawberry jelly fish.

❉ ❉ ❉

Where can you see a chorus line of cows dance the Nutcracker?

At Radio City Moosic Hall.

Little Pimple: I don't want to go to
 school today.
Ms. Zit: Why not?
Little Pimple: We're having a pop quiz.

✳ ✳ ✳

**What did Mrs. Toilet Paper say to
Mr. Toilet Paper when he started to
snore?**

 Please roll over, dear.

✳ ✳ ✳

**What kind of orange juice scares all
pimples?**

 Freshly squeezed juice.

How did Mr. and Mrs. Buttocks dance?

Cheek to cheek.

Mother: Don't worry, Son. This vaccination won't hurt.

Nurse: In which arm would you like me to stick the needle, Sonny?

Boy: In my mother's arm.

What happened to the egotistical zit?

It burst with pride.

GROSS DEFINITION
Toilet paper—
an end sweep.

Why did Paul Bunyon have a sore butt?

He fell on his big axe.

✳ ✳ ✳

What did the soap say to dirty Hans?

You're washed up around here, pal.

KNOCK! KNOCK!

Who's there?

Bee Hive.

Bee Hive who?

Bee Hive yourself while in the bathtub.

✳ ✳ ✳

Why didn't the minnow go to lunch with the stork?

He was afraid he'd get stuck with the bill.

✳ ✳ ✳

What happens when a black sheep crosses your path?

You have baa luck for a while.

Why did the gangster go to the orthodontist?
He had very crooked teeth.

✳ ✳ ✳

What military organization did Pierre the Plumber join?
The Wrench Foreign Legion.

✳ ✳ ✳

Company President: We want only urinals in our bathrooms.
Union Leader: We won't stand for a plan like that.

What do you get when Michelangelo has stomach gas?

Artsy fartsy paintings.

TONGUE TWISTED
Do Dewey and Didi do dizzy dances daily?

Why did the battery frown all the time?

It had a negative attitude.

Chester: Your uncle smells funny. How old is he?

Lester: He's way past farty.

What's black and white and blue?
A very cold zebra.

* * *

KNOCK! KNOCK!
Who's there?
Veer.
Veer who?
Veer does Mom keep the extra bathroom tissue?

Waiter: Why do you keep grunting in the kitchen?

Chef: I'm a snort order cook.

✳ ✳ ✳

Mr. Jones: My son is all grown up.

Mr. Smith: How do you know that?

Mr. Jones: Now, instead of asking me where he came from, he tells me where to go.

Cop: Should we give the press the story about the stolen toilet?

Detective: No. Let's keep a lid on it for now.

TONGUE TWISTED

Please place Petey Pooh's purple porta potty by Patty Pugh's pretty pink petunias.

Teacher: What happened to the student who swallowed his school schedule?

Nurse: One by one he's passing his classes.

❋ ❋ ❋

Why aren't filthy eggs funny?

A lot of people don't like dirty yolks.

What do you get if you cross a flock of pigeons with a herd of steer?

Roost beef.

* * *

What is the one thing pimples should never buy at the movies?

Popcorn.

* * *

KNOCK! KNOCK!

Who's there?

Bay Shore.

Bay Shore who?

Bay Shore to lift the seat before you go to the bathroom, son.

What do you get if you cross a snowman's backside with bakery rolls?

Frosted buns.

* * *

What soft drink should you put on an infected pimple?

Soda pop.

* * *

KNOCK! KNOCK!

Who's there?

Oil.

Oil who?

Oil have an accident if I don't reach the bathroom in time.

Where should you send a sick ship?
　　To see a good dock.

* * *

KNOCK! KNOCK!
　　Who's there?
Dewey Deer.
　　Dewey Deer who?
Dewey Deer go to the bathroom behind
that tree?

* * *

Blue Jay: Why do you swallow worms
　　whole?
Robin: Because when they wiggle
　　on the way down, they tickle my
　　tastebuds.

Where do you find a successful sanitation worker?

At the top of the heap.

✳ ✳ ✳

KNOCK! KNOCK!

Who's there?

Garr.

Garr who?

Garr bage day is tomorrow.

415

Home Owner: This new toilet has no
lever to make it flush.
Plumber: Don't worry. I'll handle it.

＊ ＊ ＊

**What do you call a big fight between
winged insects?**
A moth brawl.

＊ ＊ ＊

**What flies and goes "Bizt! Bizt!
Bizt!"?**
A bee with a broken buzzer.

＊ ＊ ＊

**What has four wheels, is packed
with people, and smells bad?**
Car poo.

SICK DEFINITION
Mold—
lavatory rot.

Detective: We have a lead on that stolen urinal.
Police Chief: Don't let the news leak out.

❋ ❋ ❋

How do you buy a noisy pig?
Go to a squeal estate sale.

When do you use a Japanese pay toilet?

When you have the yen to go.

✳ ✳ ✳

What do you find in a Fort Knox toilet?

Gold bricks.

✳ ✳ ✳

What do you call a happy, excited pillow?

A whoopee cushion.

✳ ✳ ✳

Why did the farm police arrest the raccoon?

He was a corn stalker.

Pooch: Hey! Let's attack that guy just for the fun of it.

Muttsy: No way! You have a sic sense of humor.

* * *

KNOCK! KNOCK!

Who's there?

Noah.

Noah who?

Noah good doctor? I have stomach problems.

419

Little League Coach: During the game, one of our baseball players threw up in his glove.

Manager: Maybe it's his vom-mitt.

Muskrat: That's the worst looking mud and stick structure I ever saw.
Beaver: Yes. It's a dam shame.

✳ ✳ ✳

Where does a three hundred pound gorilla go to the bathroom?
Anywhere it wants to.

✳ ✳ ✳

What did the stomach say to the spicy foods?
Don't cramp my style.

✳ ✳ ✳

What did the stomach say to the laxative?
We're going steady now.

DUM DUDLEY GAGS

Whit: Why are you wearing a suit of armor?

Dum Dudley: I got a job working the knight shift.

✳ ✳ ✳

Whit: In which state do the deer and antelope play?

Dum Dudley: Gnu Jersey.

✳ ✳ ✳

Dum Dudley: I got a job selling baseballs.

Whit: Are you good at it?

Dum Dudley: Yes. I have a great sales pitch.

Whit: I'm a psychic.
Dum Dudley: Well, what's stopping you
   from reading my mind?
Whit: The print is too tiny.

Dum Dudley:
   I have a
   photographic
   memory.
Whit: Then why
   do you forget so
   many things?
Dum Dudley: Can I
   help it if my mind
   isn't fully developed yet?

Whit: Dudley, how could you turn down a free trip around the world?

Dum Dudley: I wanted to go someplace else.

✳ ✳ ✳

Whit: Dudley, you're the most unpredictable person I know.

Dum Dudley: I'm not unpredictable, Whit. You just never know what I'm going to do next.

✳ ✳ ✳

Whit: Did you know I have an identical twin brother?

Dum Dudley: No. What does he look like?

Whit: My personal formula for success is hard work multiplied by opportunity.

Dum Dudley: Now that's the kind of addition I like.

✳ ✳ ✳

Whit: Just because the world is a stage, you don't have to go around acting dumb all the time.

Dum Dudley: Hey, Whit! Who's acting?

✳ ✳ ✳

Whit: What are you reading, Dudley?

Dum Dudley: It's a detective story.

Whit: That's an algebra book.

Dum Dudley: If you say so, but it's a mystery to me.

NOTICE

Dum Dudley failed his SATs because he didn't know how to make a dot.

Dudley is so dumb, he had to look up the number for 9-1-1 in the phone book.

Dudley wasn't a smart football player. He played his college ball at Notre Dum.

KNOCK! KNOCK!

Who's there?

Stu Pitt.

Stu Pitt who?

Stu Pitt is as Stu Pitt does.

Why did the police arrest the crow?

He kept making obscene caws on his cell phone.

KNOCK! KNOCK!

Who's there?

I Lloyd

I Lloyd who?

I Lloyd when I said the bathroom didn't smell bad.

Which letter of the alphabet has a bladder problem?

Pee.

✳ ✳ ✳

KNOCK! KNOCK!

Who's there?

I'm Dunn.

I'm Dunn who?

I'm Dunn using the bathroom, so you can go now.

✳ ✳ ✳

Which class is the study of urination?

Whiz Ed.

PENNY-WISE

Jenny: Do you know the name of America's national anthem?

Penny: Gosh! That's a star spangled brainer.

✳ ✳ ✳

Jenny: Will you split that minute steak with me?

Penny: Sure. You can have a second helping.

✳ ✳ ✳

Jenny: I always speak to others respectfully. I don't have a smart mouth.

Penny: It matches your brain.

GOING CRAZY

What are the directions to Diarrhea Street?

Keep going until you see a stop sign.

✳ ✳ ✳

What do you say when there's no more bathroom tissue?

Roll over.

What do you get if a sheep falls in a cesspool?

Poo on ewe.

✳ ✳ ✳

Why did the toilet paper refuse to leave the bathroom stall?

It just couldn't tear itself away from the place.

✳ ✳ ✳

Reporter: I'm trying to research material on people who don't clean up after their dogs.

Man: Oh! So you're looking for a story, but you don't want any scoops.

SICK DEFINITION
Chefs who think up chili recipes—bean brains.

What goes "Stomp! Stomp! Stomp! Stomp! Stomp! Thump!"?

A centipede with a wooden leg.

✳ ✳ ✳

What smells bad and moves slow?

A turdle.

433

Teddy: Why doesn't it do any good to write to Washington?

Freddy: Dude, the guy's been dead for years.

✳ ✳ ✳

Bob: What's it like to sell camels for a living?

Paul: It's not too bad. The work week goes fast once you get over the Hump day.

✳ ✳ ✳

Mr. Smith: I made a billion dollars installing sewers.

Mr. Jones: Oh! So that's how you got stinking rich.

Why did the toilet paper go to Hollywood?

It wanted to try out for a movie roll.

✳ ✳ ✳

What wears glass slippers and weighs 3,000 pounds?

Cinderelephant.

✳ ✳ ✳

KNOCK! KNOCK!

Who's there?

Clair.

Clair who?

Clair a path to the bathroom. I have a bad case of diarrhea.

Jack: I have diarrhea.
Mack: That's poo bad.

✳ ✳ ✳

What do you get if you cross toilet paper with a blackboard?

Something that wipes the slate clean.

✳ ✳ ✳

KNOCK! KNOCK!
Who's there?
Wart.
Wart who?
Wart do you want, stranger?

KNOCK! KNOCK!

Who's there?

Warts.

Warts who?

Warts wrong with you?

❋ ❋ ❋

Why was the sand wet?

Because the sea weed.

❋ ❋ ❋

KNOCK! KNOCK!

Who's there?

Zit.

Zit who?

Zit down and go potty for Mommy.

Why is the son of a supermarket owner more nasty than the son of a gas station owner?

The son of a supermarket owner is a little grocer.

✳ ✳ ✳

Which letter of the alphabet smells the worst?

It's stink N.

✳ ✳ ✳

What's pink and red and squishy?

A blushing tomato.

A paratrooper was making his first jump. As the plane took off, he said to Sergeant, "What should I do if I start to get airsick?"

The Sergeant stepped back and said, "Don't turn to me for advice."

439

Why wouldn't Ms. Centipede dance with Mr. Hippo?

She was afraid of getting her feet stepped on.

GROSS NOTICE

Hangman needed for gallows work—we'll teach you the ropes.

Why was Mrs. Toilet Paper so proud?

Her son was a roll model.

What do you get if you cross a skunk with Santa Claus?

A stink-ho Christmas.

✳ ✳ ✳

How do you wrap up a Christmas mummy?

Use Santa Gauze.

✳ ✳ ✳

What goes "Tap! Tap! Tap! Tap! Tap! Tap! Tap! Tap! Tap! Tap!"?

A centipede tap dancing.

✳ ✳ ✳

How do you open a cow lock?

Use a key steer.

Waiter: How did you like our tripe platter?
Customer: Frankly, I couldn't stomach it.

✳ ✳ ✳

What did Dracula say to his date?
Let's go out for a quick bite.

✳ ✳ ✳

What do you get when a space alien goes to the bathroom?
A close encounter of the turd kind.

What do you call a fat toilet?
A bath tubby.

✳ ✳ ✳

Sister: Why did you throw my high
fashion doll on the grill?
Brother: I wanted to Barbie-cue.

SIGN IN A FRIED CHICKEN RESTAURANT

All employees must wash
their hens before cooking.

Mick: You need stronger deodorant.
Rick: Hey, dude! That was a stinking remark to make.

What has four arms, four legs, and bumps into lots of things?

Two people on a blind date.

* * *

KNOCK! KNOCK!

Who's there?

Doughnut.

Doughnut who?

Doughnut get sick to your stomach in my new car.

* * *

Which letter of the alphabet has a foul odor?

E smells bad.

What did the paper towels say to the toilet paper?

Someone is always tearing me down.

What happened when the paper towels had a fight with the toilet paper?

The toilet paper got ripped to pieces.

Boy: Why are you putting dirt in boiling water?

Girl: I'm making ground coffee.

When is a pet dog good for fishing?

When it has worms.

Then there was the dirt farmer who soiled his new plants.

Then there was the pea-brained gardener who always wet his flower beds.

Then there was the stupid comb salesman who went broke because he had rotten teeth.

Man: And if I don't clean up after walking my pet dog, what then?

Cop: I'm warning you, mister! You'd better watch your step.

✳ ✳ ✳

Mr. Snoz: Ha! Ha! What a big honker you have.

Mr. Nose: Are to trying to pick a fight?

TONGUE TWISTED

Slick Sean's shiny shoes sure smell swell, sighed Sick Sue sadly.

Hal: Did cavemen make house pets out of saber-toothed tigers?

Sal: Heck, no! Where would they find litter boxes big enough?

What did the toilet paper say when it was arrested?

There's not a shred of evidence against me. I have a clean record.

❋ ❋ ❋

Which American state has the most bathrooms?

Loo-isiana.

❋ ❋ ❋

KNOCK! KNOCK!

Who's there?

Toot.

Toot who?

Toot-less people need dentures.

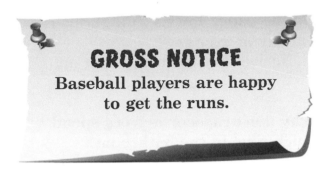

GROSS NOTICE
Baseball players are happy
to get the runs.

What happened to the famous turd?
It just dropped out of sight.

❋ ❋ ❋

Little Boy: I have a pet rodent that
loves fruit-filled pastries.
Little Girl: What do you call him?
Little Boy: Captain Hook! He's a pie
rat.

451

Do the paper towels in a public bathroom ever cry?

No, but they frequently tear up.

✳ ✳ ✳

Why don't racecar drivers spend much time in the bathroom?

They always go fast.

✳ ✳ ✳

Ben: Why are those two sheep fighting?
Len: There must be baa blood between them.

✳ ✳ ✳

Mary: I want to buy a sauna.
Carrie: Okay. Let's sweat shop.

Then there were the sloppy basketball players who dribbled sports drinks all over themselves.

Then there were the two college football teams with stinky records who played in the Toilet Bowl.

Scout: That looks like a hickory tree.
And that's an elm.
Ranger: Please don't talk bark to me.

Why is it difficult to use toilet paper in a bakery bathroom?
They have hard rolls.

What's black and white and bumpy?

A dalmation covered with mosquito bites.

✳ ✳ ✳

What waits outside a doctor's office and buzzes?

Bee patient.

✳ ✳ ✳

Why did the Hollywood toilet paper have a big ego?

It had lots of leading rolls.

✳ ✳ ✳

What goes "Hop! Bump! Hop! Thump! Bumpity-bump!"?

A wet rabbit in a hare dryer.

John: I carved an outhouse out of a tree trunk.

Clem: That's a fine whittle john.

✳ ✳ ✳

Comedian: I finish my act with an off-color joke.

Agent: If you want to be a star someday, change your dirty close.

SILENT BUT DEADLY SMILES

What would happen if you amputated your left side?

You'd be all right.

✳ ✳ ✳

What do you call a cocoon that hates social gatherings?

A party pupa.

KNOCK! KNOCK!

Who's there?

Wooden.

Wooden who?

Wooden you like a nice glass of prune juice?

* * *

What did Tarzan the Lighthouse Man name his son?

Buoy.

* * *

What did the Girl Scout leader say when she scolded her troops for throwing food?

Girls, please don't toss your cookies.

What did Mr. Hurricane say to Mr. Cyclone?

Our jobs really blow.

* * *

What did the rooster say when he went into the smelly chicken coop?

Cock-a-doodle phew!

* * *

What do you get if you cross a light bulb with a bathroom?

A watter closet.

* * *

What do you get if you put ram horns on little male rodents?

Mice butts.

GROSS DEFINITION
Seasick sailor:
A person who can't
stomach rock and roll .

What did one bowl of soup say to the other?

You've got bad broth.

❋ ❋ ❋

What's red and bumpy and green and lumpy?

A pickle with acne.

KNOCK! KNOCK!

Who's there?

Soda.

Soda who?

Soda puppy you bought is finally housebroken.

＊ ＊ ＊

Why do corporate canines use the executive washroom?

Because that's where top dogs do their big business.

＊ ＊ ＊

Snow Woman: Ick! You have dandruff.

Snow Man: Thanks for telling me now, flake-off.

Mrs. Tarzan: We built our new home in a rain forest. It has four bedrooms and tree bathrooms.

✳ ✳ ✳

What did the baseball pitcher with an upset stomach say?

I feel like I'm going to hurl any minute now.

✳ ✳ ✳

What's the difference between a gross kid and a great thinker?

A gross kid picks his nose and other people pick the brain of a great thinker.

What did one nasty light bulb say to the other?

You're not very bright, are you, dimwit?

✳ ✳ ✳

KNOCK! KNOCK!

Who's there?

Phyllis.

Phyllis who?

Phyllis glass with mouthwash and tell him to gargle.

✳ ✳ ✳

Alf: I just threw up all over my sneakers.

Ralph: How could you stoop so low?

How did the handsome movie star like his chicken dinner?

Depp fried.

✳ ✳ ✳

Father: My son had the hiccups when he was born.

Uncle: I guess he was a belching baby boy.

✳ ✳ ✳

Mr. English: Yesterday your hound dug up an herb with mildly pungent, succulent leaves in my garden.

Mr. America: Oh! You mean my dog took a leek in your yard.

GROSS DEFINITION
Nausea—
a gut reaction
to something.

KNOCK! KNOCK!

Who's there?

Dewey.

Dewey who?

Dewey have to clean the litter box right now?

KNOCK! KNOCK!

Who's there?

Police.

Police who?

Police don't eat any more Limburger cheese if you want to talk to me.

How does a duck like people to leave the toilet seat?

Down, of course.

✳ ✳ ✳

Reporter: I have a nose for news.
Editor: In that case, pick an assignment.

Why was the fussy carpenter so upset?

He had dirty nails.

✳ ✳ ✳

Son: Mom, please don't tell me that we're having chopped liver for dinner again.
Mother: Son, prepare for the wurst.

Why was the fussy horse so upset?
He forgot to polish his shoes.

✳ ✳ ✳

Why was the fussy rabbit farmer so upset?
A hare was out of place.

✳ ✳ ✳

Mother: My son Dwayne has a bad head cold.
Doctor: Is your Dwayne all clogged up?

✳ ✳ ✳

Who did Alexander Hamilbelch fight in a duel?
Aaron Burp.

Gina: My dad had echo chili for lunch.
Tina: What's echo chili?
Gina: It's a dish that repeats on you.

❋ ❋ ❋

General: Attention men! Dogs in the
  K-9 Corps are expected to go out
  onto the battlefield to do their dooty.

❋ ❋ ❋

KNOCK! KNOCK!

Who's there?

Hugh.

Hugh who?

Hugh need a stronger mouthwash, dude!

Larry: My bathroom is in great physical shape.
Cary: How do you know that?
Larry: The toilet runs all day long.

※ ※ ※

What does bald Smokey wear on his head?
A bear rug.

※ ※ ※

How do you make piggy pizza?
Prepare a regular pizza and then slop on extra toppings.

Man: Doc, I start scratching whenever
I stand next to a football, baseball,
or basketball player. What's wrong
with me?

Doctor: You have a bad case of jock
itch.

**TWISTED
DEFINITION**

Burglar—a person
who likes home
crooking.

Hal: Our new car runs on liquid animal fat.
Sal: Does it go like greased lightning?

✳ ✳ ✳

What crows in the middle of the night?
 A blind rooster.

✳ ✳ ✳

KNOCK! KNOCK!
 Who's there?
Ooze.
 Ooze who?
Ooze gonna clean up the puke in the boys' bathroom?

What do you get if you cross a motorcycle stunt driver with an insult comedian?

Wheelie gross jokes.

✳ ✳ ✳

What do you call a deformed pancake?

A flop jack.

✳ ✳ ✳

Tino: The grapes in the vineyard are refusing to be turned into juice.

Gino: What? We must stomp out this revolt at once.

What do you get if you cross a cell phone with a night crawler?

Ringworm.

* * *

How do robins prepare for a sporting event?

They do worm-up exercises.

* * *

What's worse than an elephant in a leotard?

A hippo in a Speedo bathing suit.

* * *

What do you get if you put your open mouth too close to a blender?

A really gross tongue twister.

KNOCK! KNOCK!

Who's there?

Alma.

Alma who?

Alma socks smell like stinky feet.

Police Scientist: I crossed a skin
fungus with a gang of thieves.
Detective: What did you get?
Police Scientist: A rash of burglaries.

**Why were the Joker, the Riddler, and
the Penguin standing one behind the
other?**

They were in line to use the
batroom.

BOOK ENDS

"Reduce Your Waistline"
–by Big Bill Lee

"Look Good in Loose Clothing"
–by Noah Wedgies

"Improper Digestion"
–by A. Tammy Ache

"Skin Irritations"
–by Jacque Rash

"Regularity for People on the Go"
–by Porter Potty

"Easy Bathroom Repairs"
–by Flo Problems

"How to Control Mouth Odor"
–by Xavier Breath

What kind of wood paneling is covered with icky green mucous?
Snotty pine.

※ ※ ※

KNOCK! KNOCK!
Who's there?
Butcher.
Butcher who?
Butcher dirty underwear in the clothes hamper.

※ ※ ※

What do you call Elizabeth, Victoria, and Anne before they exit the royal bathroom?
Flushing Queens.

What's the worst part of having a dinosaur for a pet?

Trying to housebreak it.

✳ ✳ ✳

Which part of a baseball game smells the worst?

The fart inning.

✳ ✳ ✳

Why did the host stop the Wheel of Fortune from spinning?

The contestant asked to take a P.

✳ ✳ ✳

What does Attila do before he takes off his pants?

He Hun zips them.

What happened to the crazy donkey?
They sent him to an ass-sylum.

* * *

KNOCK! KNOCK!
Who's there?
Ferdie.
Ferdie who?
Ferdie last time, take a bath. You really stink!